Cambridge Elements

Elements in Philosophy of Mind
edited by
Keith Frankish
The University of Sheffield

MEMORY AND REMEMBERING

Felipe De Brigard
Duke University

CAMBRIDGE
UNIVERSITY PRESS

Shaftesbury Road, Cambridge CB2 8EA, United Kingdom

One Liberty Plaza, 20th Floor, New York, NY 10006, USA

477 Williamstown Road, Port Melbourne, VIC 3207, Australia

314–321, 3rd Floor, Plot 3, Splendor Forum, Jasola District Centre,
New Delhi – 110025, India

103 Penang Road, #05–06/07, Visioncrest Commercial, Singapore 238467

Cambridge University Press is part of Cambridge University Press & Assessment,
a department of the University of Cambridge.

We share the University's mission to contribute to society through the pursuit of
education, learning and research at the highest international levels of excellence.

www.cambridge.org
Information on this title: www.cambridge.org/9781009454346

DOI: 10.1017/9781108955447

First published 2023

A catalogue record for this publication is available from the British Library

ISBN 978-1-009-45434-6 Hardback
ISBN 978-1-108-95804-2 Paperback
ISSN 2633-9080 (online)
ISSN 2633-9072 (print)

Memory and Remembering

Elements in Philosophy of Mind

DOI: 10.1017/9781108955447
First published online: November 2023

Felipe De Brigard
Duke University

Author for correspondence: Felipe De Brigard, felipe.debrigard@duke.edu

Abstract: This Element surveys research on three central and interrelated issues about the nature of memory and remembering. The first is about the nature of memory as a cognitive faculty. This part discusses different strategies to distinguish memory from other cognitive faculties as well as different proposed taxonomies to differentiate distinct kinds of memory. The second issue concerns what memory does, which is traditionally thought to have a simple answer: remembering. As it turns out, philosophers disagree not only as to how to characterize remembering but also whether the function of memory is indeed to remember. Finally, the third issue is about the nature of what we remember – a question that may refer to the object of our memories but also to their content, with different views disagreeing on how to characterize the relationship between the two.

Keywords: memory, remembering, memory trace, simulationism, episodic memory

ISBNs: 9781009454346 (HB), 9781108958042 (PB), 9781108955447 (OC)
ISSNs: 2633-9080 (online), 2633–9072 (print)

Contents

1 Introduction

The word 'memory' is polysemous. Sometimes it means information *storage*. If I say of a person that they have a good memory, I may mean that they have a sizable storage for previously acquired data. But it could also mean the very information *stored*. I may mean that they have a good memory because they have a lot of information inside the storage, regardless of its size. 'Memory' may also refer to the ability of *storing* information. I may mean that they have a good memory because they can gather lots of information or because they can do so quickly. Or it could also refer to the process of *retrieval*. I may say that they have a good memory because they are quick or efficient in bringing back to mind previously acquired information. 'Memory' could also refer to a *property* of the information itself. Perhaps I mean that they have a good memory because the information they retrieve is veridical, accurate, or faithful to the past, as opposed to false, distorted, or imprecise. Then again, 'memory' could refer to the *experience* of recollection: the 'what it is like' to bring back to mind an episode of one's past.

To complicate things, the polysemy in the term 'memory' extends beyond its folk use. Aware of these terminological difficulties, researchers are often wary of ordinary definitions and prefer instead to come up with their own. Unfortunately, such operationalizations tend to be problematic. Consider the seemingly neutral characterization of 'memory' in terms of changes in an individual's behavior as a consequence of a past experience (Crystal & Glanzman, 2013). The problem with this view is that it covers too much. I may twitch a bit after experiencing a bad sunburn, but it would be a stretch to say that I do so because I remember my past experience of sunbathing. Another common strategy is to think of memory as the capacity to remember previous experiences or information about the past. Alas, this operationalization is perilously circular, as remembering itself is often defined as that which memory does. Another approach is to define memory as the retention of internal representations of past events. Again, this characterization is problematic not only because it is unclear that memory requires a retained representation but also because one can remember events that did not occur in the past – for example, I can remember the (timeless) fact that 6 is the atomic number of carbon or that I have an appointment tomorrow.

Contemporary scientific textbooks often characterize memory as a cognitive faculty comprising three processes: *encoding*, *storage*, and *retrieval*. 'Encoding' refers to the process by means of which our memory system acquires the information it records. The maintenance of such information is called 'storage', while 'retrieval' refers to the recovery of this information when remembering. However, researchers disagree about not only the nature but also the very existence of these three alleged processes. For instance, in his contribution to a volume on memory concepts, Dudai (2007: 11) defined memory as "the retention over time of experience-dependent internal representations," yet a few pages later Moscovitch (2007: 17) argued that what is retained cannot properly be called 'memory', for – as he puts it – "memory does not exist until it is recovered." Moreover, even if we think of memory as comprising these three processes, there is little agreement as to what they are or whether they are discrete and distinct from one another. Traditionally, memory researchers thought that encoding ends and storage begins when a memory is fixed or *consolidated* in a 'memory trace'. However, there is little agreement as to how and when consolidation happens or if it occurs at all (Gilboa & Moscovitch, 2021). Another challenge comes from research showing that, at retrieval, memories can become labile and modifiable, seemingly requiring a further process of *reconsolidation* (Nader & Hardt, 2009). If so, then every act of retrieval is itself one of re-encoding, in which novel information may be incorporated into a previously stored content. Thus, the alleged independence of these three processes is questionable, as is the idea that our memories remain unperturbed from encoding to retrieval.

To complicate things, philosophers are no more consistent in their use of the term 'memory'. Not only do they disagree about its definition – they certainly do, as we shall see – but also these disagreements are often obfuscated by the lack of clarity as to what the intended target of the definition is. Consider, for instance, the debate about the distinction between memory and imagination (De Brigard, 2017). As it happens, there are at least four non–mutually exclusive senses in which memory and imagination may differ. First, one may disagree as to whether memory, qua cognitive *faculty*, is different from imagination. When discussed in this sense, 'memory' is often thought of in terms of what it does, what it is for, or the kinds of mental contents or representations it operates with. Second, one may debate whether memory qua *process*, or remembering, is different from imagining. When discussed in this sense, 'memory' is sometimes characterized in terms of necessary and sufficient conditions that make a mental act of remembering different from one of imagining and other times in terms of the sub-personal computations in which remembering, as opposed to imagining, is implemented. Third, one could disagree as to whether the *experience* of remembering is different from that of imagining. Here, to distinguish memory from imagination, philosophers often make use of notions like vividness, confidence, or particular kinds of conscious experience. Finally, philosophers may disagree as to whether a particular mental *state* is a memory. In this sense, the discussion involves alleged differences in mental contents, mental representations, or even the causal relationship to their intentional objects. Importantly, though, these different senses are somewhat independent of each other. One can hold, for instance, that remembering and imagining are different mental processes even though they are carried out by the same faculty, by separate faculties that share common processes, or by entirely independent systems. Likewise, two philosophers may agree on what is phenomenologically distinctive about memory and yet disagree on the nature of the mental contents that yield such a difference. To be fair, it is often difficult to disentangle these four senses; one's view of what remembering qua process is may be inextricably linked to one's view of what a particular memory is. Nevertheless, insofar as is possible, it is important to keep in mind the precise sense of 'memory' for which a particular view applies.

1.1 Varieties of Philosophies of Memory

Despite its centrality, the nature of memory received little attention from philosophers of mind during most of the twentieth century, and the few who thought about it approached their investigation from methodologically different perspectives. In the *phenomenological* tradition, for instance, Husserl investigated the structure and the intentionality of memory and wrote extensively on the distinct experience of remembering and its relation to our sense of time. Bergson's *Matter and Memory* (1896) also influenced phenomenologists, as it explored the notion of what is given to us in our experience of memory and recollection. Memory also plays a central role in Heidegger's *Being and Time* (1927). Building upon Husserl's realization that the experienced present presupposes the retention of an immediate bygone past and the anticipation or 'pretension' of an immediate future, Heidegger suggested that it isn't memory but forgetting that is fundamental to our experience in time. Our experienced present, when we remember, is, as it were, surrounded by a sea of forgetting. Finally, another exponent of the phenomenological approach is Merleau-Ponty (1945), who advocates for a nonrepresentational and embodied view of remembering.

Other philosophers preferred instead an *analytic* approach and conceived of their project as a semantic one, seeking to clarify the meaning of 'memory' and 'remembering' or, complementarily, the right account of the concepts of MEMORY and REMEMBERING. For instance, von Leyden (1961: 11) starts his monograph by reminding us that the philosophical question about memory is "what account to give of the concept of memory." Similarly, Martin and Deutscher (1966, 161) begin their influential paper "Remembering" by stating that they attempt to "define what it is to remember." Likewise, Zemach (1968: 526) seeks "to explicate the concept of *remembering that p* by listing the necessary and sufficient conditions for truthfully saying that S remembers that p," which in turn permits him to show "that the definition of *remembering that p* can serve as a basic definition of the concept of memory in general." But perhaps the clearest example of the analytic project is Munsat's (1966: ix) book *The Concept of Memory*, whose preface begins by denouncing the lack of a systematic analysis of the concept of memory, at a time in which "the investigation of a given concept has become all but a philosophical exercise." Interestingly, although the title suggests a positive account of the concept of memory, Munsat's book really constituted a most voracious attack on the idea that there could be such a unique concept.

In the past couple of decades, though, many philosophers have moved toward a more *inclusive* approach, as I call it, whereby not only introspective evidence from our phenomenology and conceptual analyses is considered but also empirical results from the sciences of memory – particularly from cognitive psychology and neuroscience. Philosophers working from an inclusive approach are still interested in issues such as what the nature of memory is, how to define it, or when it is appropriate to use the concept REMEMBERING. But they don't privilege conceptual intuitions or phenomenological data over scientific findings. This approach also shares a family resemblance with what Rawls called "reflective equilibrium," in the sense that philosophers working from an inclusive approach tend to go back and forth from particular (descriptive) cases – some real, some imaginary – to (normative) judgments as to whether the term 'memory' or 'remembering' should rightly be employed.

During the height of the analytic approach in the philosophy of memory, many opposed this inclusive perspective. In the preface of his celebrated book *Memory*, for instance, Don Locke (1971) admonishes that philosophers, unlike scientists, are interested in what memory consists in and thus need not be poking around brains and doing experiments, for these merely tell us how memory works, not what it is. Curiously, three centuries earlier, Descartes would have disagreed. In a letter to Mersenne, dated around November 1632, he stated that to understand what mental faculties such as memory really consist in, one needs to understand how they work, by even availing oneself of brains and such. In his words: "My discussion of man in *The World* will be a littler fuller than I had intended for I have undertaken to explain all the main functions in man. I have already written of the vital functions ... I am now dissecting the heads of various animals, so that I can explain what imagination, memory etc. *consist in*" (Descartes, 1991: 39).

Given remarks such as Locke's, one might think that the inclusive approach to the philosophy of memory is new, perhaps the product of a recent empirical turn in philosophy. I think that would be a mistake. Throughout history, philosophers have latched on to different resources to understand the nature of our mental faculties, and while some may have privileged introspective or conceptual methodologies, they too were easily influenced by both casual – and sometimes systematic – observations of memory in the wild. What is new in the contemporary inclusive account, though, is that in the past century the science of memory has developed tremendously, yielding amounts of empirical evidence far larger than anything available to philosophers in the past. The perspective from which the current Element approaches questions about memory and remembering is inclusive in this contemporary way, although it seeks to be historical as well.

2 What Is Memory?

To frame the philosophical discussion about the nature of memory qua faculty, and to understand how the different views relate to one another, I will follow the old Aristotelian structure of a *per genus et differentiam* definition (Figure 1). After all, philosophers have sought to define memory both by distinguishing it from other mental faculties, such as perception and imagination, and by differentiating distinct subclasses or kinds of memory. Unsurprisingly, however, the resultant taxonomy varies among philosophers, as do the approaches employed to distinguish them. Here, I discuss four prominent approaches (conceptual, linguistic, empirical, and phenomenological) and the distinctions they draw.

2.1 Conceptual Distinctions

The first and oldest strategy is to find conceptual, a priori, and/or theoretical reasons to differentiate memory from other mental faculties and postulate different kinds of memory. One of the first instances of this approach can be found in Plato, who distinguished between 'memory' (mnêmê/μνήμη), understood as the

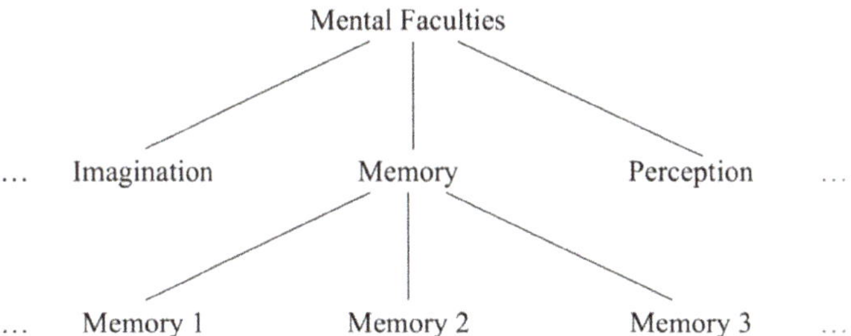

Figure 1 A *per genus et differenti(am* schema to understand the nature of memory as a mental faculty. The precise methods of differentiation vary among different views.

retention of perceptions (*Philebus*, 34a10), and 'recollection' or 'reminiscence' (anamnêsis/αναμνεσις), which played a technical role within his theory of knowledge. Aristotle likewise distinguished 'memory' from other faculties using a *content-based approach*, according to which two or more mental faculties are different from one another if the mental contents they purportedly operate upon are distinct (De Brigard, 2014a; see Section 4.1 on the notion of 'content'). Thus, memory or "the organ of the soul by which animals remember" (*Mem.* 553b5–10) is distinguished from sensation because sensations are about things in the present, whereas memories are about things in the past. Likewise, memory is different from expectation because expectations are about things that haven't happened yet, whereas memories are about things that already occurred (*Mem.* 449b25). He similarly distinguished between memory and imagination, for the latter is about things that didn't happen or are false, whereas the former is about things that did happen and are true (*De an.* 428a12–15). Moreover, the content-based approach allowed Aristotle to distinguish 'memory' from 'reminiscence', on account that the contents of the former were perceptual (*De an.* 450a22), whereas those of the latter were intellectual (*Mem.* 453a4).

Since Aristotle, others have employed content-based approaches to differentiate memory from other faculties as well as different kinds of memory. Consider Augustine who, in book 10 of his *Confessions*, wonders about the nature of memory: "A storehouse for countless images of all kinds which are conveyed to it by the senses" (§8). But then he distinguishes this kind of memory, which is imagistic, from another kind of memory where we don't retain images "but the facts themselves" (§9), such as laws of grammar or mathematics. Again, we see a difference in mnemonic content – imagistic versus non-imagistic – driving the distinction between two kinds of memory. Indeed, a case could be made to the effect that Augustine may have also anticipated a further kind of memory – emotional memory – whereby joy, sadness, and other feelings are stored (§14). This emotional memory involves bodily sensations, and it is neither imagistic nor non-imagistic but something in-between.

Aquinas, too, conceptually distinguished memory from other faculties, often following a content-based approach. To begin with, he differentiates external from internal senses. External senses (touch, taste, smell, vision, and hearing) have as their content present objects available to us in our current experience, whereas internal senses are about things that are not present. In turn, he distinguishes four internal senses depending, once again, on the contents they operate with. First, there is the *common sense* that, as in Aristotle, is the power by means of which we apprehend things as unified wholes or 'sensible forms' (which he refers to as *phantasma*). Second, there is the sense by means of which these sensible forms are retained, to which he gives the name *phantasy* or imagination (*vis imaginativa*). Third, and closely following Ibn Sina, Aquinas postulates a power of estimation by means of which we can form different judgments on sensible forms. In the case of animals, this estimative power enables them to assess, for instance, whether an approaching creature is a threat or a treat. In humans, though, because they possess intellect and will, this power to judge is not instinctual but reasoned and thus is named *cogitative sense* (*vis cogitativa*). Finally, the fourth sense is memory (*vis memorativa*), which Aquinas takes to be the repository of sensory forms for which there is a judgment or an estimation that they have been encountered in the past.

Modern philosophers, both empiricists and rationalists, to a certain extent also followed content-based approaches, although their views are so intimately connected with their opinions on the nature of remembering, memories qua mental particulars, and memory qua experience, that I am leaving some of these issues for later sections. Nevertheless, it is worth noting some instances in which a difference in content is used to help to differentiate memory from other mental faculties or operations, as well as different kinds of memory too. Take, for instance, Hobbes, who does not take sensation and imagination as two different faculties but rather as two different stages of a single process. More precisely, he notes that ideas or 'thoughts', as he prefers to call them, come primarily from sensation or 'sense', which is nothing but the representation of present objects as they impact our sensory organs. That's why ideas from the senses are not only caused by but also about present objects. Once the object is removed, though, we still retain that representation of the object, albeit less forceful than it was before. This 'decaying sense' is imagination, thanks to which we can still have thoughts about the objects that caused them despite them not being present. Intriguingly, Hobbes suggests that one can think of imagination in itself – perhaps as the mere representing of the non-present object – or one can think of it as the decay, the fading of the representation. When the decay is the focus, then, we are talking about *memory*. This is why, for Hobbes (1651/1994), "Imagination and Memory are but one thing, which for divers considerations hath different names" (1.2).

Locke's (1694/1979) views on memory are a bit more complex, but we still see him making use of the content-based approach to make certain distinctions. For instance, when talking about *Retention* (2.10), he distinguished between contemplation, or the retention of ideas for short periods of time (akin to what we may now call 'working memory'), and memory proper, which he – like Augustine – identified with the memorable moniker "the storehouse of our ideas." Again, we see the content-based approach at play, for unlike the fleeting ideas in contemplation, those in memory proper are accompanied by the additional perception that we had them before (2.10). Later, when talking about *Remembrance* (2.19) as the capacity to form ideas without the impressions or objects that gave rise to them, he distinguishes several types based on their content, including reverie, dreaming, attention, and, of course, recollection, which is the only kind of remembrance whose contents are about actual past objects or events (Copenhaver, 2017).

Locke's distinction between contemplation and memory proper is recapitulated, centuries later, by Russell (1921), who also deploys a content-based approach to distinguish between *immediate* and *pure* memory. Immediate memory referred to the retention of the immediate past, and it was perceptual, whereas pure memory referred to the retention of distant events that are no longer perceptible in immediate memory and form the basis of our knowledge of the past. For pure memory, then, belief – not perception – is of the essence. A final example of a conceptual distinction is the well-known division between *primary* and *secondary* memory, argued for by William James (1890), in which the former roughly coincides with Locke's retention and Russell's immediate memory (although with a twist, because James' notion seems to admit not only conscious ideas but also unconscious habits), while the latter comes closer to their notion of pure memory.[1]

2.2 Problems with Conceptual Distinctions

The views I just summarily reviewed constitute but a subset of conceptually motivated approaches, and they all are much more nuanced than I was able to convey. Nevertheless, they help to highlight a number of difficulties that arise when we only use a merely conceptual, content-based approach to characterize memory. A first concern with the content-based approach is that either it may fail to capture all of the relevant instances of a putative kind of memory or it may motivate the unwarranted multiplication of different kinds of memory. This is one of the lessons we learn from Munsat (1966), who criticized accounts of memory as only being about the past. As he notes, we often use 'remember' to refer to events that have not happened yet. Suppose that you leave your office with a friend, and she invites you over for a drink. "Thank you," you answer, "I'd like to very much. Oh, wait a minute, I just remember that I have to be home because Jerry is coming for dinner." In what sense, Munsat wonders, "is this 'remembering' of the past? As far as I can see, the only thing 'past-ish' about my

---

[1] Two caveats: (1) There are substantial differences in how ancient, medieval, and modern philosophers understood imagination, for not everyone took it as a 'faculty' in the same way. Alas, expanding on these nuances is beyond the scope of this Element. (2) As discussed in Section 4, Russell also employs a causal account to distinguish remembering from other mental states.

suddenly remembering that I have to do something, or be somewhere, is that we always say 'I just remembered'. But what was supposed to be in the past was *what* I remember, not the remembering" (Munsat, 1966: 5). Trying to find something about the moment in which you arranged the dinner with Jerry won't do, as the content of the memory "I remember inviting Jerry over for dinner" is not only different from the content of "I remember I have to be home in a few minutes" but also is not even necessary for you to remember anything about the moment in which you invited Jerry, or about the intention of having him over, to suddenly remember that you have to go home. All these could be causal factors leading to your sudden realization that you cannot accept the invitation, but they need not feature as the contents of your memory. Since this case appears to be a genuine case of remembering, confining memory only to contents about the past would leave out clear instances of remembering.

A possible solution is to argue that there is a kind of memory about the past and another kind of memory about, say, intentions – perhaps akin to what contemporary memory researchers call *prospective memory*. The concern with that solution is that it is possible to find other instances of 'remember' that are neither about past nor about intended events (e.g., I remember that the Pythagorean theorem is $a^2 + b^2 = c^2$), so the temptation to postulate yet another kind of memory to handle them would be conceptually irresistible. So, to prevent the proliferation of memory kinds, some additional criteria to distinguish them seems needed. This last point relates to a second concern about the use of conceptual distinctions based on mental content alone. Consider again Aristotle's claim that remembering and expecting, for instance, are distinct *because* the content of mental states that are about the past is relevantly different from the content of mental states that are about the future. What reason do we have to accept the second clause in this claim? What could prevent us from making an analogue case for, say, mental contents about things that are smaller than six feet versus things that are bigger than six feet? Why should time be a better psychological wedge than size? Even if we grant that, somehow, the considered differences in content are relevantly distinct (as opposed to the silly one I just made up), it seems as though we still need some additional reason to believe that such differences in content map onto an actual distinction in psychological faculties. One may argue that, in the case of Aristotle for instance, his theory of the mind provides the resources to justify the distinction. But then, what shall we do with the distinction once the theory is falsified or debunked? Arguably, without a theory-independent way to validate a putative content-based distinction, its validity is easily questionable.

The same argument affects other content-based approaches to distinguishing different kinds of memory. Consider Augustine's claim that memory for experiences and memory for facts are different *because* the contents of the former are imagistic while those of the latter are not. Or take Aquinas' distinction between intellectual and sensory memory, with the latter involving sensory forms and the former involving intelligible ones. Once again, what reason do we have to believe that such a distinction in content is either necessary or sufficient to dissociate different kinds of memory? What should prevent us from distinguishing memories about moving objects from memories about static ones, for instance? Again, it looks as though the answer is to be found in the theory itself. Aquinas could explain, using theoretical constructs such as 'common sense' and 'agent intellect', why in one case the contents are sensory while they are intellectual in the other. But then, what should we do when the psychological theory is proven wrong and rejected? What is the status of the distinction once the theoretical apparatus upon which it is grounded crumbles? The solution, perhaps, is to find an independent ground upon which to establish a better foundation.

2.3 Linguistic Distinctions

During most of the twentieth century, with the advent of the linguistic turn in philosophy, many conceptual distinctions were additionally supported by linguistic considerations. One of the most influential linguistic arguments to distinguish memory from imagination was based on the claim that the verb 'to remember' is factive, whereas 'to imagine' is not. More precisely, when 'remember' is used to express a relation between a subject, S, and a proposition, p, the corresponding propositional attitude report "S remembers p" can only be true if p is true. So, if one utters "Joy remembers that the mower is in the shed," the utterance can only be true if, in fact, the mower is in the shed. On the other hand, 'imagine' is not factive. One may say, for instance, "Joy imagines that the mower is in the shed," and the utterance could be true even if the mower turns out *not* to be in the shed. Arguably, this grammatical difference gives us reason to believe that memory and imagination are distinct.

Although virtually every endorser of this "factivity constraint" (Bernecker, 2010) assumes it as obviously true from the way in which competent speakers allegedly use the words 'to remember' and 'to imagine' (Malcolm, 1963; Shoemaker, 1972), at least two additional reasons have been offered in support of it. One is to argue that the conjunction of a memory claim with the negation of its embedded clause is contradictory. Thus, if someone utters

(1)   I remember I was drinking tequila, but I was not drinking tequila

then they would be contradicting themselves. By contrast, if someone were to utter

(2)   I imagine I was drinking tequila, but I was not drinking tequila

they need not be contradicting themselves. For instance, they may be talking about a day at a bar, with some friends who were drinking tequila, and they may be expressing that although they do not drink tequila – and did not drink tequila – they could see themselves as having been drinking tequila. Call this *the contradiction argument*. A second argument in favor of the factivity constraint involves the use of Vendler's criterion of factivity for the verb 'to remember'. According to Vendler (1972), one could distinguish between factive and non-factive verbs since the former, but not the latter, can be transformed into wh-clauses. A sentence like

(3)   José remembers that the car was parked

can take the interrogative forms

(4)   José remembers where the car was parked

(5)   José remembers when the car was parked.

By contrast, non-factive verbs like 'to believe' cannot be so transformed. Thus, the sentence

(6)   Ada believes that the car was parked

would render the following nongrammatical transformations:

(7)   *Ada believes where the car was parked

(8)   *Ada believes when the car was parked.

The same, *mutatis mutandis*, allegedly goes for 'to imagine'. Call this *Vendler's criterion argument*.

Linguistic differences have also been leveraged to draw distinctions between kinds of memory. A classic distinction is drawn between *factual* or propositional memory and *habit* or practical memory on account that the former is expressed by statements of the form "*S* remembers that *p*," while the latter is expressed in the form of "*S* remembers how to *q*." While primarily a conceptual distinction that harks back to Ryle's (1949) famous dichotomy between "knowledge-how" and "knowledge-that" – although, arguably, it was present in earlier writings (e.g., Bergson, 1896/1908; James, 1890; Russell, 1921) – it also found footing in linguistic considerations. Carr (1979), for instance, offered linguistic considerations to argue that a sentence such as

(9)   Lina knows that the piano is in the living room

expresses a propositional attitude, that is, a relationship between a subject, Lina, and a (true) proposition meaning that the piano is in the living room.

The particular relationship, or attitude, may vary to express a different mental state. If instead of being in an epistemic attitude of knowing that the piano is in the living room but rather in one in which Lina is perceiving that the piano is in the living room, the right expression of her mental state would be:

(10)   Lina perceives that the piano is in the living room.

By contrast, Carr (1979) argues, a sentence such as

(11)   Paderewski knows how to play the *Moonlight* Sonata

does not express an attitude toward a proposition that is able to take on a truth value but rather a different kind of relationship – one he calls *aptitude* – toward an act or an action. Thus, by parity of argument, the statement

(12)   Lina remembers that the piano is in the living room

reports a particular kind of mnemonic attitude toward the proposition – true, due to the factivity constraint – that the piano is in the living room, whereas

(13)   Paderewski remembers how to play the *Moonlight* Sonata

reports a particular kind of mnemonic aptitude toward an action that doesn't have a propositional form expressing a state of affairs in the world, and thus is not truth evaluable in the same way as propositions are but rather expresses Paderewski's ability to play the *Moonlight* Sonata.

Finally, another linguistic distinction, suggested by Bernecker (2010), capitalizes on four different kinds of grammatical constructions depending on which object the verb 'remember' takes on. First, there is *object* memory, in which the verb 'remember' takes an object as its complement, as in grammatical constructions of the form

(14)   I remember Fido

(15)   Sally remembers John.

Second, there is *property* memory, in which the direct object is a property, such as

(16)   I remember Fido's playfulness

(17)   Oli remembers the arrogance of the player.

Third, there is *event* memory, in which the verb's object expresses an action, an episode or an event, as in

(18)   I remember Fido chasing the mailman

(19)   Edgar remembers hanging the piñata.

Lastly, there is *factual* memory, in which the verb 'to remember' takes on as its complement a proposition that expresses a fact

(20)   I remember that Fido had spots

(21)   Ursula remembers that the milk expired.

Other kinds of grammatical constructions, such as when 'to remember' takes on interrogative clauses (e.g., "Sally remembers who the actor was"), are, according to Bernecker, incomplete attributions of factual memory, and thus collapse into the fourth kind.

2.4 Problems with Linguistic Distinctions

Memory taxonomies based on linguistic distinctions can be contested in several ways. Consider, first, some objections against the factivity constraint. The first one pertains to linguistic chauvinism. Let us assume, for the sake of argument, that the English verb 'to remember', embedded in a grammatical construction such as "S remembers that p," expresses a relation between a subject and a proposition referred to by a predicative that-clause. Why should that matter? According to the current edition of *Ethnologue* (Eberhard et al., 2022), which keeps track of the number of languages spoken in the world, there are currently 7,151 languages spoken today. It would be short of a miracle if all of those languages had a lexicalized verb with the exact same semantic field as the English verb 'to remember', which is also amenable to taking as direct complement sentential clauses. As a matter of fact, although probably less than 10 percent of today's languages have been decently documented (Evans & Levinson, 2009), there are already counterexamples. For instance, Dalabon, a Gunwinyguan language of the Arnhem Land (Australia), does not have a lexical verb for remembering. To express instances of remembering, Dalabon speakers use variations of past tenses and aspectual transformations on words employed to express other mental states, such as 'realize', 'attend', and 'decide' (Evans, 2007). We also have evidence of languages that do not make distinctions between verbs and direct complements, such as Straits Salish, an endangered language in the American Pacific Northwest, containing only one major class of predicative lexical item (Jelinek, 1995). Unlike the case of Dalabon, which does not contain a lexical item for 'to remember', in Straits Salish the approximate cognate of 'remembers' is not relational, at least in the same way in which it is in English. Thus, arguing for a psychological or metaphysical distinction between memory and imagination on the contingent fact that we speak English is, if not unwarranted, at least chauvinistic.

Someone may contend that the linguistic strategy pertains not to surface but to deep grammar – the underlying syntactic structure of a sentence. As such, even if a language lacks a lexicalized verb for 'remember' at the surface level, the deep grammar of linguistic expressions of remembering may still conform to the canonical structures of propositional attitude reports. Unfortunately, this strategy is still problematic, because even at the level of deep grammar, the distinction between complement, relative, and adverbial clauses is often equivocal. For example, there are cases in which is not clear whether a subordinate clause pattern conforms to one or another structure. It is tempting to interpret the sentence

(22)   I remember when I used to play piano

as taking as complement an adverbial clause. However, it is also possible to think that (22) actually expresses a relative clause with an elided head noun, such as

(23)   I remember [the days] when I used to play piano

in which case the complement isn't adverbial but sentential. The problem is that it is not obvious why (23) should be preferred rather than (22). Forcing all sentences with the verb 'to remember' to be structured grammatically as nominal phrases taking as complements sentential clauses of the form "S remembers that p" looks suspiciously like an attempt to make the data fit the theory rather than the other way around.

Others have argued against the contradiction argument for the factivity constraint. Hazlett (2010), for instance, has argued that statements such as (1) aren't necessarily contradictory; at worst, they may be incoherent, similar to the way in which Moore's well-known clause "It is raining outside but I don't believe it" is incoherent but not contradictory. The reason is simply that it is not impossible to think of a competent user who could rationally and truthfully utter a sentence such as (1). Suppose that the person that utters (1) is a tequila snob, who only considers that a tequila is *really* a tequila if it is made with 100 percent agave. Anything short of this is not tequila, according to this person, regardless of what the label says. And suppose that this person utters (1) when reminiscing about a night out, with friends, in which a cheap bottle of Jose Cuervo was opened – a bottle from which this person drank. Now we see that the first claim in the sentence – i.e., "I remember I was drinking tequila" – is to be evaluated against the speaker's intention to drink tequila and not knowing it was Jose Cuervo, which distinctively is not made with 100 percent agave, whereas the second claim – that is, "but I wasn't drinking tequila" – is to be evaluated against the value judgment that Jose Cuervo does not constitute tequila. The shifts in the evaluative conditions of these two clauses given by the context shows that (1) does not express a contradiction at all – in fact, it does not even sound that pragmatically incoherent to my ear.

Vendler's criterion argument for the factivity constraint can also be contested. First of all, while it may be true that non-factive statements containing 'to believe' cannot be grammatically rendered into wh-clauses, it isn't clear that the same occurs with all instances of statements containing 'to imagine'. Consider the following sentence:

(24)   Ada imagines that the ogre hit her on the head

whose wh-transformation would read

(25)   Ada imagines where the ogre hit her.

If Vendler criteria were true of 'to imagine', then (25) should be ungrammatical, but it need not be. Suppose that Ada is playing Dungeons and Dragons, and her character gets hit on the head by an ogre. In such a context, a sentence such as (25) is perfectly grammatical. And claiming that it isn't because Ada is imagining a *character* rather than *herself* won't work either, not only because Ada could have been playing another role-game (say, Shadowrun) in which one's imagined character is oneself but also because Vendler's argument was supposed to be about the alleged ungrammaticality of such a sentence *tout court*, not that there could be certain contexts – such as that of a role-play – in which the criterion didn't apply.

A second concern with Vendler's argument is that it is not clear what its consequences would be for our theories of memory. Suppose we accept that a sentence like (3) can be rendered grammatically into (4) or (5). Does that imply that, as a matter of psychological fact, if Jose remembers that the car was parked, then he should remember where and when it was parked? Clearly not. Jose may remember that he parked the car in the morning, but he still mightn't recall exactly where, or he may remember just the spot, but might've forgotten when exactly he parked there. It seems clear that some cases in which the wh-clauses produced by vendlerizing a statement of the form "S remembers that p" could involve information about the remembered event that need not be part of the intentional content expressed by the original statement. Are these, then, not genuine cases of remembering? If they *are*, then it is not clear what Vendler criterion is doing for us. It may be saying something intriguing about the grammar of English sentences containing the verb 'to remember', but whatever it is, it says little about the nature of the intentional contents they are supposed to express. By contrast, if we say that they *are not* genuine cases of remembering, precisely because there is some information "missing," then we are unduly constraining our cases of genuine remembering to instances in which a large amount of information about a particular event needs to be brought to mind. Many of our memories wouldn't then count as genuine cases of remembering at all.

Yet perhaps the strongest objection against the factivity constraint is that competent users of the verb 'to remember' often don't abide by it (Hazlett, 2010). Google news reports on false memories and you'll see that people feel very comfortable talking about remembering things that didn't happen or that didn't occur exactly as remembered. Moreover, recent experimental evidence suggests that in non-factive cases of implanted memories or memories of dreams participants are happy to employ the verb 'to remember' or the locution 'having a memory of', despite the fact that it goes against the factivity constraint (Dranseika, 2020). In response, philosophers typically dismiss these concerns as mere instances in which ordinary folk misuse the term 'remembering'. Specifically, they make use of the distinction between *veridical* remembering – to be used in true cases of remembering in which what is remembered did occur – and *ostensive* remembering, which is to be used in cases in which it seems as though one is remembering but one is actually not (Shoemaker, 1972). Thus, if a person utters

(26)　　　I remember that the perpetrator had a mustache

when the perpetrator did not have a mustache, then they are misusing the veridical sense of remembering when they should have used its ostensive sense, via the locution "seeming to remember." Thus, the mental state expressed by (26) should instead have been reported as:

(27)　　　I seem to remember that the perpetrator had a mustache.

Unfortunately, this common philosophical response is problematic. As noted by Schwitzgebel (2008), 'seeming' can be read in at least two ways. On the one hand, there is an epistemic sense of 'seems' that we employ to indicate doubt, hesitation, or uncertainty. On that reading, in uttering (27), I am trying to hedge, as if to indicate that I am not completely sure that what I am saying is true. But this surely is not what occurs when it comes to ordinary cases of false and distorted memories. After all, what makes many of these cases so intriguing is that, when they are experienced, people don't feel doubtful about them being memories. Thus, unless a person has a reason to be uncertain that their mnemonic experience is that of a memory, it's not clear why they should've used (27) instead of (26). On the other hand, 'seems' could be read in a phenomenological sense, perhaps to indicate something about the way in which a particular mental content is con-sciously experienced. When looking at the Müller–Lyer illusion, for example, one may say "I know that the lines are the same length, but one seems longer than the other." 'Seems' here does not express epistemic hesitation but rather something about the distinctive way in which one is consciously experiencing a perceptual content. But, again, this is not what occurs in ordinary cases of false and distorted memories, as they are typically phenomenologically indistinguishable from veridical ones. Again, unlike the case of the Müller–Lyer illusion, in which one has reason to be surprised that one line is being experienced as longer than the other, there is no such reason when it comes to ordinary cases of false and distorted memories and thus no clear motivation for having used (27) instead of (26). Philosophers who use Shoemaker's distinction between veridical and ostensive memory to summarily dismiss cases of false and distorted memories as mere "slips-of-the-tongue" aren't basing their claims on the way competent speakers use the term 'remembering' but on their unsupported commitment to the claim that 'remembering' is factive.

Finally, arguments against different kinds of memory based on linguistic distinctions are also available. It has been argued, for instance, that given a proper linguistic analysis, knowledge-how ascriptions in English can be subsumed under particular cases of ascriptions of knowledge-that (Stanley, 2011), suggesting that they may not express two grammatically distinct classes of knowledge after all. Given that linguistic distinctions between remembering-that and remembering-how piggyback on their know-that/know-how counterparts, it follows that remembering-how ascriptions could be seen as instances of ascriptions of remembering-that. Likewise, concerns about linguistic variability can also be leveraged against Bernecker's fourfold grammatical taxonomy. Werning and Chen (2017) identified at least sixteen different grammatical constructions in which the verb 'to remember' can figure in English. While these include the four forms discussed by Bernecker – object, property, event, and fact – they also include several other variants that aren't so obviously reducible to any of those four ones. So, it is possible not only that there may be other 'basic' grammatical forms of memory but also that some of those allegedly basic ones can be analyzed in terms of other variants. And lastly, and perhaps more critically, even if one were to accept that there are four basic grammatical kinds of memory in English, and even if one were to accept that somehow those four kinds replicate across all possible languages (to avoid charges of chauvinism), there is still no reason to believe that they are going to correspond to four different natural kinds of psychological phenomena. Language is very flexible, and I can easily express the exact same thought as "I remember having met you" or as "I remember meeting you," even if they correspond to different grammatical structures. Saying that because I employ different sentences I must be reporting different intentional contents gets the order of explanation backwards.

2.5 Empirical Distinctions

In recent years, the philosophy of memory has relied less on conceptual and linguistic distinctions and more on the seemingly better-grounded taxonomies of the empirical sciences. In particular, many philosophers of memory support their views on the back of the influential *standard model of memory* (SMM). Initially proposed by Squire in 1986 as a "tentative taxonomy of memory," the SMM was originally suggested to fit extant neuropsychological evidence. However, a few years later, he extended the model to accommodate not only behavioral evidence from healthy human subjects but also findings from non-human animals (Squire, 1992). For the next two decades, the SMM became the received scientific taxonomy of memory, showing up in pretty much every textbook on human psychology and neuroscience (Figure 2).

The SMM is grounded on the assumption that a sufficient condition for postulating two distinct memory kinds or "systems" is by empirically demonstrating that they can operate independently of each other – if not by double, at least by single dissociation. The keystone of the model dates to 1953 when, after a long battle with epilepsy, Henry Molaison – better known as H. M. – underwent a double resection of his hippocampi and surrounding structures in the brain's medial temporal lobe (MTL). Four years later, Scoville and Milner (1957) published his first postoperative neuropsychological assessment, and the world learned that while he showed no noticeable deficit in "perception, abstract thinking, or reasoning ability," he had developed complete anterograde amnesia (i.e., was unable to encode experiences from after the surgery) and a significant, albeit partial, retrograde amnesia (i.e., he was unable to remember many, though not all, presurgical events). In the following years, further studies helped to clarify the nature of H. M.'s neuropsychological profile, fueling the belief that his deficit was limited to long-term memory and that likely all other cognitive capacities, including perception, working memory, language, and abstract reasoning, had been spared.

These findings helped to bolster the claim not only that long-term memory relies on dedicated neural structures – that is, the hippocampus and surrounding regions of the MTL – independent of those required to exercise other cognitive faculties but also that certain kinds of memory do *not* depend on the hippocampus and, therefore, constitute distinct systems. In a classic demonstration, Milner (1962) showed that H. M. was able to improve performance in a complex mirror-tracing task. A few years later, Corkin (1968) reported similar improvements in three other motor-learning tasks: rotary pursuit, bimanual tracking, and tapping. In addition to *motor skills*, evidence also suggested that H. M. was able to acquire *perceptual skills*, such as prism adaptation, reading

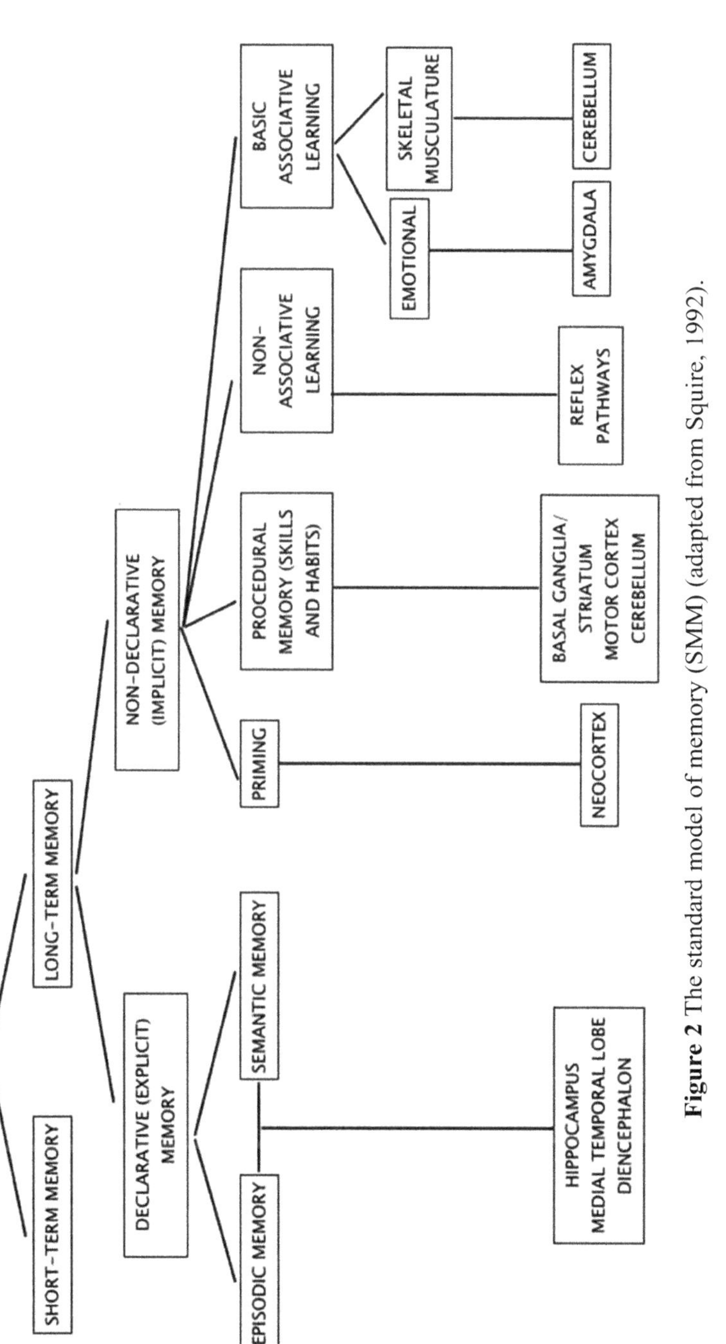

Figure 2 The standard model of memory (SMM) (adapted from Squire, 1992).

mirror-reversed words, and repetition-priming, that is, the propensity to generate perceptually and/or conceptually related responses to a previously presented unconscious prime. Critically, these observations soon extended to other patients with hippocampal damage of varying etiologies: they all showed preserved perceptual and motor skill learning with a profound concomitant deficit in their capacity to encode new information about experiences and facts. The evidence for these dissociable neural systems motivated Cohen and Squire (1980) to postulate a distinction between what they called "declarative" and non-declarative or "procedural" memory, which they likened to the aforementioned conceptual distinction between knowledge-that and knowledge-how.[2]

While strong, the evidence alluded to so far only speaks to single dissociations. Soon, though, evidence of double dissociations became available. Warrington and Shallice (1969), for instance, described the case of patient K. F., who had intact hippocampi and no impairments in long-term memory tasks but profound deficits in short-term memory. Another case is that of M. S., who had his right occipital lobe surgically removed and, after the surgery, showed no priming effects, a paradigmatic non-declarative memory task. By contrast, M. S. scored within normal ranges on all other neuropsychological tests, including declarative memory (Gabrieli et al., 1995). Similarly, deficits in statistical habit formation and motor skill learning in the absence of declarative memory impairments have been documented in patients with disorders in the striatum – for example, Parkinson's disease – but preserved hippocampi. Indeed, further evidence of dissociations between priming and motor skill learning in humans suggested that these two kinds of non-declarative memory also constituted independent kinds of memory.

Further evidence in support of the SMM came from behavioral neuroscience findings in nonhuman animals. Having demonstrated that rodents were capable of generating "cognitive maps" – that is, internal representations of the spatial layout that animals can use to navigate their surroundings (Tolman, 1940) – researchers focused their attention on understanding how these representations were acquired and where they resided in the brain. The discovery of place cells almost four decades later provided an answer: the hippocampus (O'Keefe & Nadel, 1978). As such, this neural structure, critical for declarative memory in

---

[2] Initially, the SMM distinguished *declarative* from *procedural* memory. By 1992, Squire had subsumed *procedural* under *non-declarative*, as evidence for other kinds of non-declarative memory emerged. The label 'declarative' reflected the fact that a verbal declaration was needed to verify the presence of mnemonic content in one case, while performance was needed in the other. But this nomenclature has difficulty not only accommodating data from nonverbal animals but also with the fact that one can show nonverbally that one remembers facts or events. As such, many prefer instead the labels *explicit* and *implicit*, alleging that the difference between the two is whether conscious awareness is required for encoding and retrieval of the mnemonic content.

humans, was soon associated with spatiotemporal memory in nonhuman animals. Later, in a beautiful experimental demonstration, McDonald and White (1993) showed a triple dissociation among hippocampal-dependent spatiotemporal memory, striatal-dependent habit/skill memory, and amygdala-dependent emotional memory, traditionally associated with well-known paths of fear and aversive learning. Further neuroimaging and behavioral evidence in human and nonhuman animals in the following two decades helped to strengthen the model by noting that non-declarative memory comprised four distinct memory systems: priming, procedural memory, associative learning, and reflex learning (Figure 2).

The SMM also includes a distinction, this time within declarative memory, that has received a lot of attention among philosophers, namely that between *episodic* and *semantic* memory. Reminiscent of the conceptual distinction between factual and personal memory drawn by philosophers before, the distinction between episodic and semantic memory was reintroduced in psychology in 1972 by Endel Tulving. However, unlike the evidence marshaled in favor of the other kinds of memory in the SMM, Tulving's argument was based exclusively on behavioral findings and on the consideration that the best strategy to accommodate them was by postulating two distinct computational systems. Although he acknowledged that there were a number of processes likely common between episodic and semantic memory – for example, both selectively receive and retain information from perceptual systems and can transmit information to other systems – he stressed that there were enough computational differences to think of them as distinct. Back then (although this is perhaps true of today too), at least two minimal requirements were needed to postulate a distinction between cognitive systems: (1) a difference in the nature of the information and/or representational format the system supposedly operates on and (2) a difference in the computational processing upon said representations. For example, one of the classic arguments to distinguish short- from long-term memory was based on the fact that there was a difference in the format of the representation each of the them operated with – for example, short-term memory supposedly operated with modality-specific information whereas the information in long-term memory was thought to be amodal – as well as a difference in computational processes – for example, short-term memory was capacity-limited whereas long-term memory was not.

The same logic underlies Tulving's original argument. According to him, there was an essential difference between the nature of the information stored in each kind of memory: whereas episodic memories were supposedly stored via spatiotemporal relations, information in semantic memory was stored via semantic associations. The provenance of the information was also different.

While episodic memory required "direct recording" – that is, a direct connection with the encoded mnemonic content – semantic memory involved "indirect recording," whereby the content that is encoded is not the same as the experience that brought it about. For example, one may learn that the capital of Venezuela is Caracas while having a cup of coffee in a café in Caracas, but only the memory of being in the café in Caracas is direct; the mnemonic content that Caracas is the capital of Venezuela is not identical to the experience in virtue of which it was acquired, for it is – in Tulving's verbiage – indirectly recorded. There were also putative processing differences between these two kinds of memory. Tulving argued, for instance, that retrieval made episodic memory susceptible to modification, while the same was not the case for semantic memory. Likewise, forgetting and retroactive interference – for example, when newly acquired information blocks the retrieval of previously studied items – affected episodic memory to a much greater extent than they did semantic memory (Tulving, 1983). In sum, the intuitive distinction between episodic and semantic memory that had been around for ages received, with Tulving, a new foundation afforded by the computational framework of a nascent cognitive psychology. And with it, the SMM was complete.

2.6 Problems with Empirical Distinctions

Unfortunately, accumulating research on memory in the last forty years convincingly shows not only that there is plenty of evidence against the SMM but also that some of the data used to buttress it are either cherry-picked or interpreted contentiously. Consider Tulving's episodic/semantic distinction. Shortly after his *Elements of Episodic Memory* was published, McKoon, Ratcliff, and Dell (1986) offered a series of careful and detailed criticisms of the very same studies Tulving used to support an episodic/semantic distinction. They point out, for instance, that the experiments he mentioned in support of differential effects of interference between episodic and semantic memory suffered from serious dissimilarities in demand characteristics in the experimental designs, making it impossible to fully assess the alleged difference between conditions. Likewise, they argue that Tulving's interpretation of the neuropsychological data on individuals with amnesia is flawed and that, if anything, extant evidence shows parallel deficits in semantic and episodic memory. Indeed, even the famous case of K. C., who also suffered bilateral damage in his hippocampal and parahippocampal areas, doesn't evidence double dissociation between episodic and semantic memory, as it is not at all clear that his semantic memory is preserved. Similar criticisms were leveled against other alleged distinctions, including both in informational format and in computational processing. Moreover, in that very paper, McKoon and colleagues cite many existing studies, not mentioned by Tulving in his discussion, which – according to them – provide empirical counterevidence against the claim that the distinction between episodic and semantic memory has a strong empirical footing. Today, probably no expert believes that episodic and semantic memory are independent cognitive systems, and the precise ways in which they interact constitute an active area of scientific research (De Brigard, Umanath, and Irish, 2022).

There is also ample evidence against other dissociations postulated by the SMM. Indeed, some of this counterevidence comes from a careful reading of H. M.'s neuropsychological and experimental data. First, contrary to popular belief, H. M.'s retrograde amnesia was much more profound than textbooks acknowledge. In a comprehensive follow-up profile of H. M., Corkin (1984) reports that he didn't really seem to have autobiographical memories from the eleven years prior to his surgery and that most likely he could only remember *two* events prior to that: one about his first cigarette and another involving a plane ride. Thus, the idea that H. M. did not have retrograde amnesia is rather doubtful. The SMM also asserts that one needs an intact hippocampus to encode new semantic information, a claim often supported by H. M.'s alleged incapacity to learn new facts. However, noticing that H. M. was often able to fill crossword puzzles with cues referring to facts that occurred after the surgery, O'Kane and colleagues (2004) demonstrated that H. M. could recognize the faces of individuals who became famous after his surgery and in the vast majority of cases he could also indicate why they were famous. Additional studies conducted by Corkin herself also suggest that, albeit slowly, H. M. was able to encode new factual and conceptual information (Corkin, 2013). Moreover, the idea that H. M. showed normal skill learning is at best exaggerated, if not utterly false. As mentioned, by the early 1960s, H. M. had been tested on a single mirror-tracing task supposedly tapping skill learning. And in this task, which asked him to trace a star-shaped figure by only looking at the reflection of his hand holding a pen, H. M. showed a marked reduction in errors and faster reaction times over thirty-nine trials in the course of three days. But soon after, he was tested on a sequential maze-task, which was also supposed to measure skill learning. His performance, however, was abysmal. Even the simplest version of this task, which took controls less than twenty trials to fully master, was completely impossible for H. M. (Milner, Corkin, & Teuber, 1968). The results aren't much better for rotary pursuit and bimanual tracking, both tasks in which he was asked to hold a metal-head stylus against moving target points. In both tasks, H. M.'s performance was never on a par with controls, taking many more trials, and making many more errors, than even the worst-performing control subject. Indeed, Corkin (1968) herself mentions in the discussion that it would be a mistake to think that H. M.'s skill performance is unimpaired, and she even went on to suggest that skill learning likely requires our capacity to learn facts – an observation that goes strictly against the backbone of the SMM (De Brigard, 2019).

Other neuropathological cases provide counterevidence as well. One of the precepts of the SMM, for instance, is that an intact hippocampus is required to learn any new declarative information. But this does not seem to be the case. The patient characterized by Warrington and McCarthy (1988), for instance, showed normal memory for the meaning of both premorbid and postmorbid words. Further counterevidence comes from three well-documented cases of childhood hippocampal amnesia (Vargha-Khadem et al., 1997), all of whom, despite being profoundly impaired in their capacity to recollect past personal experiences, were nonetheless able to complete high school – an unthinkable feat unless they were capable of learning new factual information. Other neuropsychological cases cast doubt upon another central claim of the SMM: that short- and long-term memory are distinct because only the latter, and not the former, depends on the hippocampus. As it happens, while it seems as though short-term memory for individual words and digits may be unaffected by MTL amnesia, it is rather impaired when it comes to remembering conjunctions of items, faces, scenes, and topographical landmarks (Ranganath & Blumenfeld, 2005). Moreover, and contrary to what's assumed by the SMM, MTL damage affects other domains outside of memory, including certain perceptual discrimination, episodic future and counterfactual thinking, and even social cognition tasks.

Finally, recent behavioral and neuroimaging evidence strongly suggests that the alleged dissociations captured by the SMM are either unclear or plainly false. For instance, consistent with the neuropsychological data, several studies have shown hippocampal engagement during certain working-memory tasks in both human and nonhuman animals (Ranganath & Blumenfeld, 2005). Likewise, many neuroimaging studies report hippocampal activity during tasks other than declarative memory encoding, including perceptual discrimination, spatial navigation, and episodic future and counterfactual thinking (Schacter et al., 2015). Critically, there is also evidence showing clear engagement of the hippocampus and MTL during motor skill learning, which is in direct contradiction with a central tenet of the SMM. Finally, there is also quite a bit of behavioral and neuroimaging evidence showing strong neural overlap between tasks that were supposed to recruit entirely distinct neural structures. In a useful review piece, Dew and Cabeza (2011) argue that there is significant neural overlap in tasks indexing conceptual priming, which is typically associated with non-declarative memory, and tasks indexing familiarity, which is normally associated with episodic memory. They also review several studies showing not only that the hippocampus is more sensitive to previously presented information – relative to new information – but also that these effects are independent of whether the information was consciously encoded or not. That the hippocampus is recruited during the encoding of unconscious episodic information goes against the very characterization of declarative memory assumed by the SMM.

The evidence just mentioned constitutes the tip of an ever-growing iceberg of findings that directly contradict the SMM. Contrary to what many philosophers assume, there is more and more consensus in the scientific community to the effect that the SMM is wrong and, more importantly, that it is starting to lose its usefulness. As a result, in the last ten years or so, researchers have proposed different taxonomies that arguably fit the evidence better. Reder and colleagues (2009), for instance, suggest reinterpreting the explicit/implicit dichotomy, not in terms of awareness but in terms of the strength of the activation and degree of binding of the components in the mnemonic content. Henke (2010), instead, proposed a new model of memory systems with only a tripartite division based on the nature of the encoding and retrieval processes as well as the neural architecture that supports them. And more recently, Murray, Wise, and Graham (2017) offered an entirely different taxonomy of memory systems – the evolutionary accretion model – based on their different phylogenetic histories. Thus, far from being the received view, the SMM is increasingly questioned.

2.7 Phenomenological Distinctions?

In addition to conceptual, linguistic, and empirical distinctions, philosophers sometimes discuss taxonomies based on phenomenology. After all, and as I will discuss at length in Section 4, philosophers have regularly employed phenomenological differences (e.g., vivacity, familiarity) to try to distinguish remembering from perceiving and imagining. However, nowadays there is an influential view that has employed phenomenological distinctions to draw a taxonomy of kinds of memory. As mentioned, up until the mid-1980s, Tulving had consistently characterized episodic memory in computational terms. But, in 1985, he put forth a different way of distinguishing episodic, semantic, and procedural memory according to which these three memory systems are nested and hierarchically structured and are discernible by the nature of the consciousness they are associated with. Procedural memory, which stands at the basis, is associated with *anoetic* consciousness, whereby the organism is only aware of its present and immediate surroundings, while remaining utterly unaware of anything outside its current situation. Next up is semantic memory, associated with *noetic* consciousness, which allows the organism to be aware and act upon symbolic and conceptual relations inherit in the information recalled. Finally, on top, there is episodic memory, which he now associates with *autonoetic* consciousness, a kind of awareness that "confers the special phenomenal flavor to the remembering of past events, the flavor that distinguishes remembering from other kinds of awareness, such as those characterizing perceiving, thinking, imagining, and dreaming" (Tulving, 1985, 3). Thus, on this view, it is thanks to episodic memory that we can properly remember, in the sense of becoming autonoetically consciously aware of events that occurred in our personal past.

Although Tulving introduced this taxonomy as highly speculative, the truth is that his initial computational characterization of episodic memory was slowly deemphasized in favor of his new way of characterizing it in terms of autonoetic consciousness. Unfortunately, far from making the distinction clearer, I think the introduction of a consciousness criterion muddled the waters even more. First, the proposal emerged as a way of describing the phenomenological experience of patient K. C. and thus many of Tulving's claims had the evidential weight of mere conjectures. Indeed, when characterizing the nature of autonoetic consciousness, he said that the lessons learned from K. C. enabled him to "speculate about the general nature of autonoetic consciousness" and offer a "tentative list" of six of its properties – all of which, time and again, have been challenged (Tulving, 1985, 5). For instance, he suggested that autonoetic consciousness enables one to mentally travel in time from one's past to one's possible future. But recent research suggests that properties of autonoetic consciousness are also evident when individuals engage in episodic *counterfactual* thinking (De Brigard & Parikh, 2019). He also suggested that autonoetic consciousness was necessary for episodic remembering, which meant that there couldn't be instances of episodic memory without autonoetic consciousness. However, some neuropsychological cases have been described in just such a way, namely as individuals that can remember concrete personal episodes from their past without feeling the phenomenological characteristics associated with autonoetic consciousness (e.g., Zeman & Butler, 2010). And never mind questions about the phylogeny and ontogeny of autonoetic consciousness, for Tulving suggested that since nonhuman animals and human infants lack autonoetic consciousness, then they must lack episodic memory too. Finally, he thought that autonoetic and noetic consciousness were experimentally measurable by employing strategies such as the remember/know paradigm, whose validity has been widely criticized (Umanath & Coane, 2020).

2.8 Assessment

We started off this section hoping to characterize memory qua faculty following a *per genus et differentiam* strategy. We then followed philosophers' preferred approaches to demarcating differences between memory and other cognitive faculties, on the one hand, and within different kinds of memory, on the other, and we found them all lacking. For our purposes, there are two consequences that follow from this discussion. First, I think it is about time to accept that memory does not form a natural kind (Michaelian, 2011) and that it does not correspond to a system entirely distinguishable – on conceptual, linguistic, empirical, or phenomenological grounds – from other alleged cognitive faculties such as perception or imagination. Although the orthodoxy of faculty psychology is as endearing as it is enduring, I think it is about time to reject it. We need to accept the fact that our biological makeup is such that different cognitive operations frequently deploy common mechanisms to solve tasks across domains traditionally thought of as conceptually distinct. But, second, this does not mean that philosophy of memory can't be done on a solid footing. On the contrary, despite the difficulty of characterizing distinct kinds of memory, most authors have no trouble when it comes to identifying paradigmatic cases of memory or remembering. Often, progress is made not thanks to the production of an account of a particular phenomenon in terms of necessary and sufficient conditions, or even thanks to the careful drafting of an experimentally useful operationalization, but rather by way of offering *deictic* definitions: denoting the extension of a term by pointing at an instance of proper use. Come to think of it, this is often how we, as researchers, start off: we give a deictic definition of the phenomenon in terms of an illustration or particular case – "think about the experience of remembering the cup of coffee you enjoyed this morning" – and then we proceed with an account (if we are philosophers) or an operationalization (if we are scientists) under which that particular case must be subsumed. I say, don't. Forget about the account; just think about the case.

3 What Is Remembering?

In addition to wondering about what memory is, philosophers are also interested in understanding what memory does – an inquiry typically approached as a question about the nature of *remembering*. Given how many different kinds of memory philosophers have postulated, it is natural to think that there are also different kinds of remembering. Surprisingly, though, most philosophical discussions have been confined to the nature of what can be called – for lack of a better term – *episodic* remembering, whereby the content of one's memory is a particular past event or episode that the person experienced. Our discussion will thus be limited to different views on episodic remembering – although it is worth noting that there is increasing interest in other kinds of remembering, such as remembering skills and emotions and even collective remembering (Michaelian & Sutton, 2017). And, once again, Aristotle is a good starting point.

Recall that, following the content-based approach, Aristotle takes memory to be different from perception because the former is about the past while the latter is about the present. But, then, he wonders (*Mem.* 450a25), how could it be possible that something that is not present – the remember*ed* – could nonetheless be the content of a mental state that is present – the remember*ing*. His answer builds upon Plato's, who compared remembered experiences to seal rings leaving impressions in a wax table (*Tht.* 191d). Likewise, Aristotle thought that, when we remember, what we presently perceive is an image of a past event. Yet Aristotle notices that this simple answer raises the following concern: if what happens when we remember is that we perceive an image of a past event, should we then say that what we remember is the image or should we rather say that what we remember is the past event the image is an impression of (450b11)? Each solution is problematic. If we say that what we remember is the current image, then we are forced to say that what we remember is present. But this cannot be so, for memory is about the past, and the past is not present. However, if we say that what we remember is past, then how could it be possible that we can perceive that which is not present? Perception is, by definition, of what is present, and the past is, well, not present. Aristotle's solution to this dilemma is clever and, in a sense, profoundly influential. With Plato, he accepts that remembering involves the creation of an impression of a past event. But then he highlights that this impression should be understood not simply as an image but as a "copy" or *eikon* of a past event, meaning that it should both *resemble* the event and be directly *caused* by it (450a27–b11; Sorabji, 1972). As such, for Aristotle, to remember consists in to presently perceive a preserved mental representation of a past event that both resembles and was caused by it.

I say that Aristotle's view is profoundly influential because it gives a general structure to both classical and contemporary discussions on the nature of remembering. First, his view takes remembering to be a three-stage diachronic process. The first stage consists in some kind of imprinting that takes place when the remembered experience occurs – the making of the *eikon*, if you will. The second stage is the retention of the imprinted *eikon* – the *memory trace* – which carries the content of the remembered experience through time. And third, there is the recovery or reinstatement of the memory trace during recollection, whereby one becomes aware of its retained content and thus remembers the past experience. Now, if you pick a textbook in cognitive psychology or neuroscience, chances are it describes remembering as involving precisely these three stages, likely with the monikers *encoding*, *storage*, and *retrieval*. And chances are it characterizes *encoding* as the process by which information is stored in memory, *storage* as the process by which information is maintained, and *retrieval* as the process by which stored information is recovered. In fact, this E–S–R model of remembering is not that different from some of the most influential philosophical views of remembering for the past two millennia. Consider Augustine, for instance, for whom memory is a storehouse where we keep the images of our senses: "Each experience enters by its own door [the senses], and is stored up in the memory. And yet the things themselves do not enter it, but only the images of the things perceived are there for thought to remember" (10.12–13). Sensory experience leaves images of that which is perceived in storage, as it were, for us to retrieve and remember past things by.

Augustine's image of memory as the storehouse of ideas was later resurrected by Locke in the first edition of his *Essay Concerning Human Understanding* (1689). He thought that memory was the part of the mind in which past perceptions remained hidden from consciousness until they were further revived in the act of recollection. But he soon recanted that view because it blatantly contradicted one of the main tenets of his theory of ideas: there are only conscious ideas. If memory stores ideas one is not aware of, then the mind can have unconscious ideas, which – for Locke – is absurd. So, Locke amended his view with one of the most oft-quoted passages of the second edition (1694) of his Essay:

> But, our ideas being nothing but actual perceptions in the mind, which cease to be anything when there is no perception of them; this laying up of our ideas in the repository of the memory signifies no more but this: that the mind has a power in many cases to revive perceptions which it has once had, with this additional perception annexed to them, that it has had them before. And in this sense it is that our ideas are said to be in our memories, when indeed they are actually nowhere; but only there is an ability in the mind when it will to revive them again, and as it were paint them anew on itself, though some with more, some with less difficulty; some more lively, and others more obscurely. (10.2)

Thus, when it comes to remembering, Locke's view belongs to a family of views I call *classical representationalism*. There are two characteristics that unify these views. First, they all take remembering to be mediated by a mental representation or memory trace whose content is a past event or perception. Second, they sought to distinguish cases of remembering from other mental processes involving mental representations via an *internalist* criterion, that is, a phenomenological marker by means of which one could tell whether the experience is a memory or not.[3] As I will discuss in Section 3.3, contemporary

---

[3] *Classical representationalism* is sometimes referred to as "The Empiricist Theory of Memory," thanks to Holland (1954). But this is a misnomer for, as explained in Section 4, many rationalist philosophers held representationalist views on memory that were almost indistinguishable from their empiricist counterparts.

versions of representationalism tend to favor externalist criteria – typically causal criteria – as well as some variations in the nature of the intermediate memory representation. But to get to that, we need to discuss classical representationalism first.

3.1 Classical Representationalism

One of the first proponents of this family of views was Descartes, who sought to establish a distinction between remembering, perceiving, and imagining on both biological and phenomenological grounds. He suggested, for instance, that while the brain activity underlying perception is similar to what occurs when we remember and when we imagine, there is a difference in degree of *liveliness* among them: "The impressions that come into the brain through the nerves are usually more lively and more distinct than those stimulated in the brain by the spirits" (Descartes 1649/1985: 338). Perceptions are more lively than memories, which in turn are more lively than imaginations. In addition to liveliness, Descartes also suggested a second internalist criterion: coherence. Relative to merely imagined events, experiences of actual remembered events cohere better with our beliefs (*Meditations*: vii, 89–90). Thus, Descartes' classical representationalist view is one in which perceiving, remembering, and imagining are processes mediated by impressions, and whose differences are to be found internally, in the way in which the contents of the relevant impressions are experienced.

Almost contemporaneously, Hobbes was advocating for another representationalist view. Inspired by the notions of motion and inertia, Hobbes thought of our sensory impressions as being the effect of objects on our senses. When we see an object, its motion is hindered by our eyes and as an effect it leaves a sensory image. As long as the object is seen, its effect endures and the image is clear. But if the object is removed or we close our eyes, its effect decays and the image loses clarity. Imaginations and memories are, therefore, faded sensory impressions, which led Hobbes to famously declare, "Imagination and Memory are but one thing" (Hobbes 1651/1994: 7). Yet Hobbes thought that remembering was different from imagining thanks, again, to another internalist criterion: the purpose for which we use those faculties. If our goal is to bring to mind "simple imaginations" – that is, images as they were perceived, unchanged, by the senses – then we are remembering. But if our purpose is to conjure up "compound imaginations" – that is, images composed of simple imaginations pieced together – then we are imagining.

In the following decades, both modern empiricist and rationalist philosophers offered different internalist criteria for distinguishing remembering from imagining and perceiving. The typical strategy was to argue that memories are accompanied by a *memory marker* at retrieval. Spinoza, for instance, thought of memories as being accompanied by a thought about their past duration, which is remarkably similar to Locke's own version of memory marker, namely that, when we remember, we revive ideas with the "annexed perception" that we had them before. This strategy continued to be popular even in the nineteenth and early twentieth century, as both James (1890) and Russell (1921) suggested their own memory marker. Yet arguably no internalist criteria for distinguishing remembering from imagining was as influential as the two suggested by Hume. The first criterion was vivacity: "The ideas of the memory are much more lively and strong than those of the imagination" (Hume, 1739/1978: 1.1.3). The second criterion involved the structural preservation of the original impression at retrieval: "Imagination is not restrain'd to the same order and form with the original impressions; while the memory is in a manner ty'd down in that respect, without any power of variation" (1.1.3). Hume, however, was aware of the obvious difficulties of the second criterion: one simply cannot bring back to mind the original impression to compare it with the retrieved one, so he placed more importance on the internalist criterion of vivacity (1.3.5).

Nevertheless, Hume's vivacity criterion has been widely criticized. Ryle, for instance, argued that Hume's use of the terms 'vivacity' or 'lively' was ambiguous and wrong. On the one hand, Hume may have meant by those terms something like 'life-like', and thus it makes sense to say that a realistic looking plastic doll is livelier than a rag doll. But, according to Ryle, this use makes no sense for mental representations. On the other hand, Hume may have meant by those terms something like 'intensity', so that memories are more intense than imaginations. But, again, Ryle thinks that such meaning also makes no sense for imaginations, for while a sensation can be said to be stronger or weaker than another, the same is not the case for images: "While I fancy I am hearing a very loud noise, I am not really hearing either a loud or a faint noise; I am not having a mild auditory sensation" (Ryle, 1949: 269). Another influential criticism, which emerged time and again, was clearly stated by Holland (1954: 269): "The suggestion that the haziest of recollections must be somehow clearer and more vivid than the most powerful products of a lively imagination seems implausible, if not senseless." Holland explores two versions of this objection. The first version pertains to *individual* memories. According to this version, Hume's vivacity criterion states that *all* memories are more vivid than *all* imaginations. Thus, for every particular memory, m, and every particular imagination, i, m is more vivid than i. However, it is a fact that, sometimes, a particular i is more vivid than a particular m. Therefore, it is not the case that all *m*'s are more vivid than all *i*'s.[4] The second version takes Hume's vivacity criterion as suggesting that, *on average*, memories are more vivid than imaginations. However, Holland argues that the notion of 'average' makes no sense in the case of memory and imagination, as there is no measure according to which the ranges of vivacity can be compared, the same way in which, say, weight can be compared to make claims to the effect that, on average, things made of lead are heavier than things made of cork – even if some things made of cork are heavier than some things made of lead. Without a common measure of vivacity for memory and imagination (akin to weight), not even this second reading of the criterion survives.

Finally, it is worth mentioning Urmson's attempt to safeguard Hume's vivacity criterion. According to Urmson (1967), there is an ambiguity in the way 'imagining' and 'remembering' are used in this discussion. On one hand, imagining and remembering can differ in terms of their success criteria. One may successfully imagine something when one attempts to invent something freely and does it. Conversely, one may successfully remember when one attempts to bring to mind a past experience and does it. In this sense, Urmson suggests, Hume was right in taking the internal character of the mental activity as sufficient criterion to determine whether one is imagining or remembering. However, if 'imagining' and 'remembering' are understood in terms of accuracy, then internal criteria won't work, as we can't simply tell, from the subjective experience alone, whether what we take to be a memory is or is not an accurate representation of what happened, just as we can't tell whether what we are imagining does, in fact, correspond to an actual past event. Furlong (1970), alas, is not convinced, for he believes that Urmson is making Hume draw a distinction he did not have in mind: that of *attempting* to imagine versus *attempting* to remember. Furlong correctly points out that such was not Hume's intention and, therefore, that Urmson's strategy isn't an adequate defense of Hume's internal criterion of vivacity.

3.2 Nonrepresentationalism

Some difficulties of classical representationalism were noted initially by Reid (1785/1849), who proposed one of the first nonrepresentational views of remembering, in part, as a response to Locke. According to Reid, if an idea ceases to exist during a certain period of time after which it is revived, then it has

---

[4] Hume anticipated this objection when he claimed that sometimes a memory, "by losing its force and vivacity, may degenerate to such a degree, as to be taken for an idea of the imagination; so on the other hand an idea of the imagination may acquire such a force and vivacity, as to pass for an idea of the memory, and counterfeit its effects on the belief and judgment" (1.3.5). But he thought these rare cases were no threat for his view.

two beginnings, namely when it first appears in consciousness and when it is later recalled. But, as Locke himself asserted, one and the same thing cannot have two different origins. Therefore, all Locke is allowed to say is that memory can create a *new* mental representation that, at most, resembles the previous one. But resemblance isn't enough for a representation to be a *memory* representation. There are lots of images – including mental images – that resemble previous ones without being memories.

> Every man knows what memory is, and has a distinct notion of it: but when Mr. Locke speaks of a power to revive in the mind those ideas, which, after imprinting have disappeared, or have been, as it were, laid out of sight, one would hardly know this to be memory, if he had not told us. There are other things which it seems to resemble at least as much. I see before me the picture of a friend. I shut my eyes, or turn them another way; and the picture disappears, or is, as it were laid out of sight. I have a power to turn my eyes again toward the picture, and immediately the perception is revived. But is this memory? No, surely; yet it answers the definition as well as memory itself can do. (Reid, 1785/1849: 3.7)

Somehow we need to recognize that the second idea is, or is very much like, the first idea we had before. Unfortunately, this act of recognition presupposes memory. Therefore – Reid argues – Locke faces the problem of either accepting that one and the same thing can have two origins or having to admit that his definition of memory is circular.

A second problem for representationalism has to do with the cause of a memory representation. If remembering consists in reviving representations formerly contemplated in perception, and if those representations were caused by the objects affecting our senses, what are then the causes of our memories of those objects? One possibility is to say that the objects themselves cause our remembering them. Unfortunately, since those objects are in the past and our remembering is in the present, then the causes would be temporally disconnected from their effects – which, for Reid, was inadmissible. Alternatively, one could claim that something other than the objects themselves cause our remembering them. But then, why would such remembering be precisely about their objects? If there is no causal or, at least, nomological connection between the remembered object and the content of the memory representation one perceives when remembering, then we may open the door to skepticism for there won't be any reason to guarantee that one's memory is indeed about the represented object. Memory representations just don't come wearing any epistemic warrant on their sleeves. Finally, Reid also criticized Hume's version of representationalism on similar grounds, in addition to being one of the first critics of the vivacity criterion as a reliable strategy to differentiate remembering from imagining (Reid, 1785/1849: 2.289).

3.2.1 Direct Realism

Reid's counterproposal – often called *naïve* or *direct realism* – is to get rid of the notion of an intermediate mental representation altogether and to think instead of memory as "immediate knowledge of things past" (Reid, 1785/1849: 2.253). When it comes to perceiving, our mind is directly and immediately acquainted with its object by the exercise of our faculty of perception. Likewise – the argument goes – when it comes to remembering, our mind is directly and immediately acquainted with its object by the exercise of our faculty of memory. The only difference between the object of perception one is acquainted with when perceiving and the object of memory one is acquainted with when remembering is that the former exists in the present while the latter exists in the past. But this difference alone isn't sufficient to require us to postulate intermediate representations. Thus, when we remember, we don't retrieve a mental representation whose contents are past things but rather we get to be in direct contact with the past things themselves.

Direct realism regained popularity at the beginning of the twentieth century. Laird (1920, 51) for instance, defined remembering as "the mind's awareness of past things themselves," rather than of any sort of "present representations of past things." Likewise, Stout (1930) argued that there is no difference between the memory-image of a remembered experience and the remembered experience the image is supposed to be a representation of; both are one and the same. Similarly, Woozley (1949: 62) held that to remember is for our mind to be in direct contact with the "actual event remembered," not with a memory image of said event. The memory images one may experience when remembering are not constitutive of the act of remembering and shouldn't "be regarded as entities at all" (63), for what matters for remembering is the cognitive relation involved, which is between the mind and the past thing itself, as the image of the past event "is not a thing at all distinct numerically from the thing remembered" (64).

Nevertheless, direct realism has been widely criticized. One concern is that direct realists who consider remembering tantamount to perceiving usually suggest that their only difference is that remembered objects are in the past whereas perceived objects are in the present. But remembering is also phenomenologically different from perceiving. Memories, for instance, are coarser than perceptions. While we may be pretty good at visually discriminating very similar shades of red when perceived simultaneously, for example, we would be much worse if we were to rely solely on memory. Or, to use a case from Furlong (1951), suppose you are trying to remember your neighbor's new garden gate, and you are asked "how many vertical bars does the gate contain?" Although you may be willing to reject certain answers as wrong – definitively is more than three and certainly less than twenty – you likely can't remember the exact number. Now, were you to perceive it, all you'd have to do is to count them. The gate, after all, is right there in front of you. Why can't you do the same when remembering if you are supposed to be in direct contact with the past itself? At least two possible responses are open to the direct realist. One possibility is to say that, in addition to a difference in the object, there is also a difference in the nature of the relation toward the object and that this second difference somehow accounts for the asymmetry in our experiences. But then the burden is on the direct realist to give an account of the nature of that relation such that it can explain phenomeno-logical differences that occur not only between remembering and perceiving but also between different instances of remembering, such as the fact that we may remember a particular event more vividly at one time versus later on. Another possibility is for the realist to explain the difference in experience in terms of a difference in the nature of the object itself: the present-gate when perceived is different from the past-gate when remembered. But this makes the nature of the past objects one is supposedly presently related to when remembering even more mysterious. How come the gate we see in the morning is different from the one we remember in the afternoon? And how come the former had a determinate number of bars while the latter doesn't? Again, the direct realist owes us an explanation of the mysterious nature of such presently existing past objects.

A second criticism concerns false and distorted memories (Furlong, 1948). As an illustration, consider a classic study conducted by Loftus and colleagues (1978), in which participants were shown a series of thirty color slides, each for three seconds, depicting the successive stages of a car accident. Importantly, half of the participants saw one slide with a car stopped at a 'stop' sign, while the other half saw a 'yield' sign; otherwise the slides were the same (Figure 3). After a twenty-minute distraction task, participants were given a memory questionnaire about the car accident. Now, one of the questions asked participants whether they remember the car stopped in front of a 'stop' sign. Critically, half of the partici-pants that saw the 'yield' sign received this question, while the other half received the same question but with the 'yield' sign instead; ditto for those who saw the 'stop' sign. Thus, half of the participants in each condition received a misleading question. After several iterations of this general design, the authors found that a substantial portion of participants – in some experiments more than 50 percent – falsely remembered having seen the car stopped at the sign they did not see in the slides. How should the philosopher of memory explain this phenomenon? A representationalist could readily explain it as a simple case of misrepresenta-tion, but that's not a resource available to the direct realist. What would they say then? One possibility is to say that while those participants who correctly remembered, say, the 'stop' sign are directly acquainted with the past event that

Figure 3 Critical slides used in the presentation sequence
(from Loftus et al., 1978).

includes a 'stop' sign, those that remembered the 'yield' sign are instead directly acquainted with another, counterfactual past event that includes a 'yield' sign (for this kind of response, see Woozley, 1949). The problem with this response is that it makes the acquaintance relation even more mysterious, for it looks as though it can relate us not only to existing past events that actually occurred but also to existing counterfactual ones that did not. In sum, the oddness of the cognitive relation of remembering as well as that of the direct objects postulated by direct realism may be too steep a price to pay in exchange for representations.

3.2.2 Behaviorism

In addition to direct realism, there is another family of nonrepresentational views on remembering I may hesitantly call *behaviorism*. Inspired by Wittgenstein's animosity toward the use of mental representations to account for psychological processes, the behaviorist account of remembering suggests that there is no need to invoke a memory trace, even if there is such a thing as a neural modification that occurs in virtue of experiencing an event, in order to understand the concept of remembering. Amidst his cryptic remarks on memory, Wittgenstein seems to have held at least two reasons to drop the use of memory traces to account for remembering. The first one had to do with his notion of memory content. For Wittgenstein, to remember is a success term; you either remember or you don't. Whether there is a particular kind of experience that accompanies an instance of remembering, it isn't essential to it. "Memory-experiences are accompaniments of remembering," he says, for "remembering has no experiential content" (Wittgenstein 1953: 2.13.231). Given that what is experienced introspectively isn't constitutive of remembering, the idea that memory requires a temporally continuous memory trace bearing such an experience as its content is, for Wittgenstein, absurd: "Whatever the event does leave behind in the organism, it isn't the memory" (Wittgenstein, 1980: 1.220). As such – and this is his second reason for rejecting the idea of a memory trace – there is no need to require an intervening memory trace as a causal factor in our explanations of remembering:

> I saw this man years ago: now I have seen him again, I recognize him, I remember his name. And why does there have to be a cause of this remembering in my nervous system? Why must something or other, whatever it may be, be stored-up there in any form? Why must a trace have been left behind? Why should there not be a psychological regularity to which no physiological regularity corresponds? If this upsets our concepts of causality then it is high time they were upset. (1.905)

The idea that a successful account of remembering doesn't require the postulation of a causally relevant memory trace was further elaborated by Malcolm (1963) and served as part of the motivation for the contemporary representationalist version of causal theory. According to him, a successful account of remembering need not refer to any intervening causal story, let alone any invocation of memory traces, occurring between the witnessed event and its recollection. As we will see, though, the influential causal theory of remembering, which I discuss in Section 3.3.2, is in part a direct response to Malcom's views on remembering (and I will also explore his views on memory traces in Section 4). But before that, there is another theory we need to discuss first.

3.3 Contemporary Representationalism

The difficulties with classical representationalism and direct realism led some philosophers to reconsider the need for intermediate representations to account for remembering. But what is represented in memory, as well as the notion of a memory representation itself, varies among theorists. Additionally, unlike classical representationalism, contemporary versions of representationalism tend to postulate external criteria for a mental process to count as remembering, as opposed to imagining. Since this continues to be an active area of research in the philosophy of memory, I will limit my survey to the most influential views in the last few decades.

3.3.1 The Epistemic View

Dissatisfaction with intermediate memory images did not always lead to non-representationalism. One attractive alternative was to consider them as mere prompts to the content that actually gets stored in memory, namely a *belief* about the experienced event (Ayer, 1956). Now, since remembering was assumed to be factive, the stored belief was also considered to be true – presumably justifiably so – and thus memory beliefs were taken to be a particular kind of knowledge. According to this *epistemic* view, when I remember that the dryer was running this morning, I am doing so in virtue of having acquired in the past a (justified) true belief that the dryer was running this morning, I have kept that belief since I formed it, and I am now entertaining it as I am recalling that fact. In a nutshell, then, for the epistemic view to remember that p is to know that p, where this knowledge was previously acquired and preserved. Barring variations among different alternatives, the epistemic view typically postulates at least four conditions for S to count as remembering that p (Bernecker, 2010):

(1) S knows that p at t_2
(2) S knew that p^* at t_1
(3) p is identical with, or sufficiently similar to, p^*
(4) S's knowing at t_2 that p is suitably connected to S's knowing at t_1 that p^*.

The first condition states that the subject presently knows some particular fact about their past, say, that they had coffee at breakfast. The second condition states that the subject also knew that fact in the past – for instance, they knew, in the morning, that they were having coffee. The third condition states that the content of the subject's knowledge state in the present – for instance, that they had coffee in the morning – is identical (or sufficiently similar) to the content of their knowledge state in the past – for instance, that they're having coffee, at breakfast. Finally, the fourth condition states that there is a suitable connection between the contents, that is, between the knowledge, in the morning, that they're having coffee, and the knowledge, now, that they had coffee then.

The dialectic among partisans of the epistemic view often involves counter-examples to one or many of these conditions, and subsequent amendments to try to safeguard a knowledge – or at least a belief-based – account of remembering. Gettier-like examples, for instance, have been proposed to challenge the present knowledge and the past knowledge conditions, and others have argued that, given empirical evidence to the effect that memory errors and distortions are common and ubiquitous, the content at t_2 cannot be identical to that at t_1, and thus offer different accounts of similarity to try to preserve the mnemonic content (Bernecker, 2010; Frise, 2015). However, I am going to largely sidestep these debates, because my concern here is the extent to which the epistemic view captures not so much the epistemology but the nature of remembering itself. Specifically, the question is whether taking beliefs as the carriers of the representational content – as opposed to memory images – can successfully account for what remembering is. And the answer, to anticipate, is that they likely cannot.

A first set of concerns with the epistemic view pertains to the scope of the view. Typically, the epistemic view is couched in terms of propositional knowledge, whereby the content of the memory belief is a proposition expressed by embedded that-clauses. Unfortunately, as we saw in Section 2.4, it is unlikely that such memory statements are generalizable across languages or pick out real psychological kinds of memory. Additionally, it isn't clear that episodic memory can be understood propositionally, if propositions involve concepts as their constituents. It has been argued, for instance, that the fact that I can notice at retrieval information I hadn't been consciously aware of at encoding, when presumably the initial belief formation took place, indicates that there are nonconceptual contents in our memories that may be hard to accommodate by a propositional account (Martin, 2001). Moreover, even if one were to limit the propositional account to nonpersonal memories, as opposed to personal or episodic memory, it is unclear that such a category neatly identifies a real psychological process (Michaelian & Sutton, 2017).

The second – and, in my view, more pressing – reason to reject the epistemic view concerns psychological tractability. Leaving aside the fact that propositions are notoriously difficult to accommodate within a naturalistic worldview or provide much theoretical help when it comes to explaining a variety of memory phenomena uncovered by the science of memory, the epistemic view faces serious challenges when one scrutinizes the nature of memory beliefs more closely. Let us think, for a second, how and when exactly the memory belief in (1) "S knows that p at t_2" is formed. And, to put it more concretely, let us consider again the Loftus et al. (1978) study mentioned in Section 3.2.1 (Figure 3). Suppose that you are a participant, that you were in fact presented with the slide showing the 'stop' sign and suppose further that you *do* remember the car stopped at the 'stop' sign. How would the epistemic view go about explaining the phenomenon? Presumably it would say that, when you saw the slide, you formed a belief with the content that the car stopped at the 'stop' sign. But when did that happen? Did it happen at the beginning of the three-second exposure of that particular slide? Or did it happen at the end? But, if so, were you forming the belief alongside your perceiving the next slide? Did the two cognitive processes conflict or did they run in parallel? How? And how long did it take you to form the belief? One second? Two seconds? Or the whole three seconds of exposure of the next slide? Did forming the belief about the particular episode of the car stopped at the 'stop' sign take the same amount of time as seeing the episode, or did it take less time? If less time, did you still get to store all the perceptual information that impinged your senses during the three seconds of seeing the slide, or did you just encode part of it? If all, how did the informational compression happen?

To traditional philosophers, these may appear to be purely rhetorical questions. But I think they aren't. If we want the epistemic view of memory to be able to explain the nature of remembering, it needs to give us an account of the precise nature of the belief content represented, how it gets fixed, when, and in what format. Philosophers tend to discuss examples in purely abstract terms – "*S* believes that *p* at t_1," and so forth – but when we try to apply these formulas to actual instances of remembering in the real world, the theory loses track of the phenomena, for it is not clear how it is that we go about the world doing two things in tandem: experiencing it and forming beliefs about it. Or perhaps we do, but the theory is not transparent about how this could occur, in the real world, in minds like ours. Incidentally, this concern also applies to scientific views that take perceiving and encoding as two separate processes, without really explaining how and when one ends and the other begins. At any rate, many philosophers take for granted the vocabulary in which the epistemic view is couched, perhaps because it is a remnant of good old-fashioned semantic ascent:[5] we attribute mental states to others in terms that, superficially, seem like "S-[intentional-verb]-that-*p*," and we assume that the underlying reality fits that structure. Yet this assumption is seldom questioned. Not only that; we seldom question whether such an underlying structure is truly the best one to give an answer to traditionally difficult questions in the philosophy of memory, such as whether we can trust our recollections, whether truth, accuracy, and fidelity depend on one another, and so on. Either way, I think more work is needed for the epistemic view to offer more than an incomplete account of the nature of remembering.

3.3.2 The Causal View

Classical representationalism advocated for internal criteria – memory markers – to distinguish remembering from perceiving and imagining. By contrast, the causal view suggests an external criterion: an appropriate causal connection between the remembered event and the remembering. More precisely, the causal view – popularized more recently by Martin and Deutscher (1966) – holds that an individual remembers a past event when (1) they represent the event at the time of retrieval, (2) they represented the experienced event at the time of encoding, and (3) there is an appropriate causal connection between the content represented at encoding and the content represented at retrieval (Michaelian & Robins, 2018).[6]

---

[5] Roughly, the move from talking about things to talking about the way we talk about things.

[6] The causal theory is neutral about the nature of the representation. Martin and Deutscher (1966) required the content stored in the memory trace to be a structural analogue of the experienced event. But this requirement is consistent with a variety of formats, including imagistic but also, in principle, propositional. Bernecker's (2010) view, for instance, is a mix of causal and epistemic view, as he takes the format of the representation to be belief-like.

The addition of the qualifier 'appropriate' is essential for the view, as it rules out instances of relearning, whereby an individual represents a certain event, then forgets its, but then reacquires the same representational content through some other way – someone's testimony or hypnosis, for example. The thought here is that such cases are not instances of remembering, as the causal chain from the experience of the remembered event to the process of remembering is deviant, not appropriate. And what makes it appropriate is that the represented content is carried by a memory trace, formed at encoding, stored unchanged during the elapsed interval from encoding to retrieval, and causally 'operative' at the time of retrieval, when it is remembered.

Much of the motivation for the causal view was to distinguish cases of actual remembering from cases of apparent remembering and of apparent imagining. To see how this works, consider a modified version of the Loftus et al. (1978) experiment I mentioned in Sections 3.2.1 and 3.3.1. Suppose that, in addition to being asked whether you remember having seen the car stopped at the 'stop' sign, you are asked to sketch the content of your memory. Thankfully, you are a gifted artist and can reproduce faithfully what comes to your mind. Having been in the group presented with the car at the 'stop' sign, and having brought to mind a representation of the car stopped in front of the 'stop' sign, you produce a drawing identical to the panel on the left-hand side in Figure 3. Unquestionably, you do remember the car stopped at the 'stop' sign – which the causal theory readily explains by telling us that you remember the episode because you represented it when you first saw the slide, you then stored a memory trace with the content you represented when you saw the slide, and now, when you are asked about it, that very memory trace caused the represented content to be consciously accessible to you and, thus, remembered.

Now recall that half of the participants saw the slide depicting the car at the 'stop' sign, while the other half saw a 'yield' sign. And, as it happens, roughly a third of those who were shown the slide with the car stopped at the 'yield' sign wrongly reported having seen the car stopped but at the 'stop' sign. Suppose now that you were in the group that saw the 'yield' sign, and when you are asked if you remember the car stopped at the 'stop' sign, what comes to mind is a representation depicting the image in the left-hand panel of Figure 3. As a result, you answer the question affirmatively and sketch a drawing identical to the image in the left-hand panel. You are then among those who misremembered having seen the car at the 'stop' sign while in fact they saw it stopped in front of a 'yield' sign. The causal view tells us that this wouldn't be a case of remembering, for the content you were aware of at retrieval was not brought about by a representation with the same content as what you saw when the slides were presented, and thus whatever you represented then was not causally operative in bringing about what you represented and drew at retrieval, as both contents are distinct. Importantly, the theory also explains cases of apparent imagining that turn out to be cases of genuine remembering. Consider the following variation of the painter's case discussed by Martin and Deutscher (1966). Suppose you are shown the image of the car stopped at the 'stop' sign but then, for whatever reason, you forget having seen it. Sometime later you are asked to draw an imagined picture of a car by a 'stop' sign but, when doing so, you bring to mind a representation just like the one you've been presented with before. As a result, you draw a picture identical to that in the left-hand panel of Figure 3. The intuition here is that it would be very unlikely that you'd have come up with that exact same image unless you'd actually seen that slide before. Not unlike instances in which suspects are incriminated for revealing details of crime scenes unlikely to have been known by someone who wasn't there, the causal theory would consider your experience of apparent imagining as one of remembering – perhaps tantamount to instances in which individuals remember an episode but forget its source.

While the causal view slowly became dominant in the philosophy of memory, several opposed it on different grounds. One line of criticism, which I will discuss in Section 4, rejects the notion of memory trace endorsed by the view. Other concerns pertain instead to the necessity and sufficiency of conditions (1) to (3). Against sufficiency, we can think on the one hand, along with Debus (2010), that our personal memories are epistemically relevant to us in a way that nonpersonal memories aren't, and thus that a condition conferring some kind of epistemic authority to representations of past experienced events would need to be added for the causal view to be successful. Similarly, one could think that in addition to the aforementioned three conditions, we may still need to add a subjective or phenomenological one, stating, for instance, that only mnemonic representations that are accompanied by autonoetic consciousness can count as personal memories, as nonpersonal memories or personal memories devoid of autonoetic consciousness don't play the same role as episodic memories in our cognitive economy (Dokic, 2014). On the other hand, arguments against necessity can focus on the assumed requirement that memory traces need to carry intentional content, as opposed to being merely representational vehicles, from the experienced event to the episode of remembering (Werning, 2020). Alternatively, one may argue against the assumption that memory traces need to bear explicit contents and hold instead that what they carry is the capacity to instantiate a process or a procedure, acquired at encoding, that brings about the remembered content at retrieval (Perrin, 2018). Or finally, and more critically, one could challenge the need for a causal condition at all.

3.3.3 The Simulation View

The necessity of an appropriate causal connection between the remembered event and the episode of remembering has been challenged recently by the simulation view – an approach largely motivated by two strong lines of empirical evidence. First, a wealth of research in the past few decades has convincingly demonstrated that remembering is often inaccurate, distorted, and false. Even memories we take to be true, and upon which we act and live our lives seamlessly, are often imprecise or flatly wrong. Yet false memories aren't entirely haphazard; there is an air of plausibility to them, as they are typically not entirely inconsistent with either the individual's background knowledge or the conditions of encoding. For instance, in a classic study, Brewer and Treyens (1981) asked participants to wait in a regular academic office while the experimenters were setting up the experiment. In reality, however, the office was the experimental setting. Each item in the office was carefully placed and catalogued; some were objects one would typically find in an office – that is, items consistent with the 'schema' of an office (e.g., stapler) – while others were clearly inconsistent (e.g., a beach ball). After a short wait, participants were escorted out to a different room where they received a surprise memory test in which they were asked to remember, from a list of objects, which ones were in the office they were just at. The list included both items that were present in the office and items that were not present or 'lures'. The results revealed that participants were more likely to endorse as remembered or to 'false alarm' to lures that were schema-consistent relative to schema-inconsistent ones.

A similar influential study, conducted by Roediger and McDermott (1995) based on a previous design by Deesse, shows that when participants are presented with a list of semantically related words, they tend to false alarm to semantically related, as opposed to unrelated, lures. Indeed, the air of plausibility in false memories extends to more 'ecologically valid' settings, such as a famous experiment in which Loftus and Pickrell (1995) managed to generate a false memory of having been lost in a shopping mall in about a third of their participants. While unlikely, having been lost in a shopping mall as a child was not an altogether implausible event for most participants, and evidence suggests that the less plausible the event, the less likely one may falsely remember it as having occurred (Garry et al., 1996).

But if remembering is to accurately reproduce past perceptions, why would we have a memory system that produces so many false alarms? And why would these false alarms occur so easily, so frequently, and so systematically? Some researchers argue that this evidence is better explained if we think of memory not as reproductive but as constructive (Schacter, 2008; De Brigard, 2014b): what we do, when remembering, is not to retrieve the exact same content stored when the event was experienced but rather to construct a mental simulation aimed at depicting it, employing stored information that may or may not have been acquired during the experience of the represented event. Why would remembering be constructive in this way? The answer to this question comes from a second line of research that has inspired the simulation view.

In his seminal work, Talland (1965) characterized Korsakoff's amnesiacs as being unable not only to remember the past but also to make future plans. Years later, Tulving (1985) would describe similar difficulties in another famous amnesic case, K. C. Indeed, this observation prompted Tulving to think of episodic memory as a capacity within a larger cognitive system for "mental time travel," thanks to which we are also able to engage in episodic future thought. In the last twenty-five years, the view that our capacity to remember our personal past and imagine a personal future are profoundly intertwined has received substantial confirmatory evidence from many scientific fields, including neuropsychology, cognitive neuroscience, developmental psychology, and neurophysiology of humans and nonhuman animals (Schacter et al., 2015). Moreover, further studies have extended the mental time travel view to also show that common neural mechanisms are also involved in imagining episodes of a possible personal past that could have occurred but did not – that is, episodic counterfactual thinking (De Brigard et al., 2013; De Brigard & Parikh, 2019). Thus, taken together, these two lines of evidence – one on false memories and one on episodic past, future, and counterfactual thinking – motivated some philosophers (De Brigard, 2014b; Michaelian, 2016) to reject the causal condition and the claim that memory is reproductive, in favor of a constructivist account in which remembering is a particular instance of a more general capacity to mentally simulate personal episodes that may occur in a possible future or could have occurred in a possible past. The most precise articulation of the simulation view, put forth by Michaelian (2016), could be condensed in the following formula (Michaelian, 2022): a subject, S, remembers an event, e, if and only if (1) S now represents e and (2) S's current representation of e is produced by a properly functioning and hence reliable episodic construction system that aims to produce a representation of an event belonging to S's personal past.

There are a few alternative ways of cashing out this formula. The one I favor interprets the reliability of the system in computational terms.[7] At the heart of this

---

[7] Michaelian's own interpretation is along the lines of reliabilism in epistemology, whereby the system is reliable if it consistently produces true beliefs. Reliabilism is the target of several concerns, some of which have to do with generality. My sense is that, to avoid these concerns, Michaelian's reliabilism would need to be understood in computational terms. As such, my interpretation here is not only consistent with Michaelian's but also seeks to offer a mechanistic/computational foundation to his.

interpretation lies the fact that we live in a world that constantly offers way more information than we can store. Moreover, the information that reaches our senses is scattered and filtered by our attention and likely more is lost during encoding and, no doubt, by time and decay. Yet, when we remember, the contents of episodic memories we experience as successful recollections come to us whole, even when some of their details may be blurry, missing, or imprecise. Given the amount of informational loss from encoding to retrieval, how do we manage to generate memories of full-fledged past episodes, often with a force so evocative that it makes us feel as though we are almost reliving them? The simulationist's answer is that, as long as the system is working well, it will seek to construct a mental simulation whose content would depict as accurately as possible the past event. Importantly, the simulation view of remembering can readily explain the two aforementioned lines of research. On the one hand, the engagement of common neural regions during episodic past, future, and counterfactual thinking occurs because those same computational constructive processes are deployed during these three kinds of mental simulations. On the other hand, the prevalence of schema-consistent false memories in ordinary life is explained by the fact that while most of the time the mental simulation constructed by our memory at retrieval is such that it accurately represents the targeted past event, sometimes it does not. Yet the computational operations underlying the constructive process are equivalent in both cases.

The simulation view is thus not committed to the causal claim insofar as it does not make it necessary for a genuine memory to include as its content the very same information that the subject experienced in the past and is now remembering. Sure, often enough the (massively filtered) encoded content will play a role in the construction of the mental simulation of the remembered event, but sometimes it won't. A genuine memory could just as well be produced by the same computational processes without the need to include information caused by the original event. The occasional memory of an event that did not happen, as well as the who-knows-how-frequent episodic memories of actual personal events generated by contents not acquired during the remembered experience, are, for the simulationist, as bona fide memories as those whose contents are fully or even partly constructed out of information stored when the remembered episode was experienced.[8]

---

[8] I am painfully aware that I am sidestepping the very complex issue of understating the proper use of adjectives such as 'genuine', 'true', 'veridical', and 'accurate' in the context of causal and simulationist theories of memory. Some causalists may say, for instance, that a retrieved content that is experienced as an episodic memory but is brought about by a deviant causal chain can be veridical, albeit not genuine, remembering. By contrast, a simulationist may be happy saying that a computationally reliably constructed content that accurately depicts a past personal experience counts not only as genuine but also as veridical remembering even if there is no causal connection

Rejecting the causal condition and the factivity of remembering and questioning the nature of contentful memory traces may appear counterintuitive, yet the simulation view has the advantage of fitting the empirical evidence as well as the phenomenology of false memories and mental time travel better than the causal view. Nevertheless, in the past decade, philosophers have leveraged a number of difficult objections to the simulation view. Some have argued, for instance, that innocuous cases of misremembering should not be conflated with instances of maladaptive confabulation but that the simulation view cannot tell these apart (Robins, 2016a) and that only a fully (Bernecker, 2017) or partially causal view (Robins, 2017) can account for the difference (but see Michaelian 2016, 2020). Robins (2016b) also points out recent evidence showing that certain neuronal interventions, such as optogenetic stimulation, can generate the kinds of false memories the simulation view is supposed to be fit to explain. However, her careful exploration of the neural mechanisms underlying optogenetically generated false memories shows that constructive views have a much harder time than causal views when it comes to explaining these findings. Others have argued that there are metaphysical differences between episodic memory and future thinking, such as the fact that the objects of episodic future thoughts are general while those of memories are particular (Debus, 2014) or that the relationship between the subject of the experience in a memory is fundamentally different from that of the projected subject in a future thought (Perrin, 2016). More recently, Robins (2020) has forcefully argued that while there are indeed similarities between episodic memory and other kinds of mental simulations – particularly episodic future and counterfactual thinking – there are critical empirical and phenomenological differences that likely outweigh their commonalities and, as a result, she offers a picture of memory and imaginative simulations as being discontinuous with one another that seems to fit better and more of the available empirical evidence. Needless to say, the debate between the causal and the simulation view is very much alive. While some have argued for hybrid proposals (e.g., Robins, 2016; Langland-Hassan, 2022), it is likely that the best solution may involve the rejection of some of the terms of the debate – or so I will argue at the end of Section 4. But before we get to that point, there is an important detour that will help to clarify this debate further.

3.4 Coda: What Is Memory For?

In his influential *Manual of Psychology*, the psychologist and philosopher G. F. Stout claimed that the function of memory is "merely reproductive" and that it does not involve the transformation of the revived ideas "in accordance

---

between the past event and the retrieval process. Unfortunately, a full treatment of these issues will have to wait for a separate work.

with present conditions, [as such revival] requires the objects of past experiences to be re-instated . . . in the order and manner of their original occurrence" (Stout, 1899). Little seems to have changed during most of the twentieth century, as philosophers kept assuming that what memory does is to remember and that to remember is to reproduce the past. False and distorted memories, however occasional, were taken as instances of a malfunctioning faculty whose true purpose was to reproduce the past with fidelity (Kurtzman, 1983). But because of the accumulating empirical evidence on forgetting rates as well as on the prevalence of false and distorted memories, researchers started to question whether we may have been wrong about not only what memory does but also what it is for.

One of the first attempts to carefully question the reproductive function of memory came from the computational psychologist John Anderson (1989, 1990), who argued that the systematicity of our memory errors, and the trajectory of our forgetting rates, could be understood when taking into account the computational limitations of the informational retrieval system our memory is. Here is a cartoon version of a kind of memory we could have had – call it *Funes' memory*, after Borges' fantastic character (Borges, 1944). In Funes' memory, every detail from every single experience – whether a perception, a dream, a thought – is immediately stowed, without any loss of information, with full fidelity, in an infinite storage. Memories are individually *archived* – to use Robins' (2016) apt term – in such a way that they are immediately retrievable when needed. Whether the memory is of an obscure event one was barely aware of decades ago or a recent salient experience that was just put in storage, both retrieval time and accuracy are identical. Remembering, in Funes' memory, consists in an informational retrieval problem, for which a particular kind of strategy offers the optimal solution.

Alas, our memory is not at all like Funes'. Again, much of the information that reaches our senses is never consciously perceived, and much of the contents of our conscious experiences are not encoded at all. Storage is also likely massively overlapping and distributed, so individual memories are not neatly and separately put away. We also forget – a lot – and at different rates depending on the nature of the information, the age of the memory, and the conditions of encoding. And, of course, retrieval is very complex: sometimes it is fast, sometimes slow, certain cues are more effective than others, and accuracy and vivacity vary greatly. In sum: our memory, unlike Funes', is noisy and uncertain. As a result, the strategy for retrieval is going to be different in a memory like ours. Given these computational limitations, we need to understand how such a noisy and uncertain system can still manage to solve an informational retrieval problem in a way that is adaptive for us.[9] Anderson's proposal starts from the assumption that we need accurate information about the past for future purposes. Retrieving an accurate memory, then, constitutes a gain, although the process of retrieval itself is costly. Consequently, our retrieval strategy is going to be one in which we can maximize the odds of a gain – for instance, the odds of a successful and accurate retrieval – and minimize the odds of a cost – for instance, failing to retrieve an accurate memory or retrieving an inaccurate one. Anderson's model was initially concerned with optimal solutions for memory encoding, and was largely focused on specific effects in semantic memory, but has been so profoundly influential in the cognitive science of memory that many promising extensions of his "rational analysis of memory" have been offered for retrieval and episodic memory (Gershman, 2022). I will get back to Anderson's proposal in Section 4.3, but for now it is enough to say that it was a watershed moment in the sense that it forced memory researchers to seriously reconsider the nature of remembering by inviting us to rethink what memory may be for in minds as noisy and uncertain as ours.

The sacrosanct notion that memory is for remembering, and that remembering consists in the reproduction of encoded contents at retrieval, was once again questioned by Glenberg (1997) in what should have been a more influential article. Inspired by the in-vogue embodied cognition mentality of the late 1990s, Glenberg recognized the importance of the body and of our spatial embeddedness in the world for informational retention. Perspectival and spatial information tends to be better remembered than the same information in pretty much any other format, and sequences of embodied actions tend to increase retention more so than any other orderly strategy. Remembering, from Glenberg's perspective, consists in the mental simulation of embodied trajectories that allow us to predict behaviors and fine-tune courses of action. Perhaps, then, it isn't so surprising that by the time 2007 came around, and with it a surge of several experimental pieces showing neural overlap in episodic memory and future thinking (Addis et al., 2007; Hassabis et al., 2007; Suddendorff & Corballis, 2007; Szpunar et al., 2007), the ideas that memory's function may not be to faithfully reproduce the past, that what conferred its adaptiveness was the probability of it being needed for future use, and that its contents were akin to ersatz experiences or 'simulations' were already well established in many

---

[9] An annoying terminological issue in much of the literature on the function of memory is that the term 'adaptive' is often employed to mean 'beneficial for the organism,' which is different from its meaning in evolutionary biology. A trait can be beneficial for an organism without it being adaptive for the species the organism belongs to. Arguing for the etiological function of a trait on the basis of token as opposed to type adaptiveness is tricky. Readers interested in this debate should be cautious of how the terms are employed.

cognitive scientists' minds. As a result, the proposal – initially put forth by Tulving (1985) and further articulated by others (e.g., Atance & O'Neill, 2002; Klein et al., 2002) – that episodic memory is but an operation of a larger system for mental time travel gained further steam.

Now philosophers took notice, and partisans of the simulation view suggested not only a different account of remembering but also an alternative view of the function of memory; rather than it being an individual mental faculty for the reproduction of past experienced contents, memory became a process of a larger system for mentally simulating possible personal events in order to improve future behavior (De Brigard, 2014b; Michaelian, 2016). Neurally, the system was thought to correspond to the brain's default mode network, a set of functionally and anatomically connected brain regions that reliably comes online when we engage in cognitive tasks involving mental simulation of possible personal events, such as episodic past, future, and counterfactual thinking (Schacter et al., 2015). The fact that the same neural structures are involved in these varieties of episodic simulation – of which episodic memories are but a subclass – helps to explain not only why these cognitive abilities tend to develop in tandem but also why they tend to follow parallel paths of decay due to both pathological and non-pathological etiologies.

Recently, however, several philosophers have raised concerns about this functional view. Some have argued, for instance, that the traditional account of memory's function as reproduction allows for deviations of literal recall and, thus, can accommodate evidence from the systematicity of false memories, thereby undercutting some of the motivation for the alternative functional view (Schwartz, 2020). More recently, Aronowitz (2023) argued that the process of semantization – whereby episodic information slowly adopts a semantic structure – threatens the distinction of episodic and semantic memory and thus the idea that episodic, but not semantic, processes are part of a single system for episodic simulation. Finally, and more critically, Robins (2022) points out that sameness of neural structures is not sufficient – and likely not even necessary – evidence for a common evolved function, as it often happens that the same brain structures are redeployed to perform different functions in different contexts (Anderson, 2015). Additionally, accumulating evidence shows that the brain's default mode network is engaged in a large number of cognitive (and, I would add, purely metabolic) operations that do not neatly square with the alleged functions of an episodic simulation system. Moreover, Robins suggests that once we deemphasize the neural similarities – which could be accounted for by mere redeployment, rather than a common function – and emphasize the many documented differences, it becomes clearer that episodic memory is distinct from other kinds of imaginative simulations and thus should not be thought of as a mere process within a single future-focused cognitive system.

Alternative functional proposals have been put forth recently by other authors. One such proposal is that memory evolved for communication and to help us track epistemic authority over our own as well as others' beliefs (Mahr & Csibra, 2018). Knowing who has firsthand, as opposed to secondhand or mere hearsay, knowledge of a particular event is, allegedly, vital to exercise epistemic vigilance over our conspecifics, helping us to learn who to trust and who to avoid. More recently, Boyle (2022) argued for an expanded mnemonic model of memory that moves beyond the traditional reproductive account without being committed to the future-oriented function favored by the simulation view. According to her view, and consistent with the traditional approach, memory evolved to help us encode, store, and retrieve information; however, contra the traditional approach, she argues that the relevant information isn't merely episodic and personal but rather something akin to the more general knowledge that is typically associated with semantic memory. Accordingly, episodic memory did not evolve as a single system, or even as a suboperation of a single system for episodic simulation, but rather as a gateway to encode, store, and retrieve semantic information within the more general faculty of declarative memory.

Although the debate about the function of memory is fairly new, we already have learned a number of things. A first lesson is that while the inquiry about the nature of memory qua faculty can be pursued largely independently of questions about what remembering is and what memory is for, their answers tend to be profoundly intertwined. Knowing why we evolved the kind of memory we have may influence our answer as to what remembering consists in or how to individuate memory from other cognitive faculties. A second lesson is that researchers are not always clear as to what they mean by 'function' (Schwartz, 2020; Schulz & Robins, 2022). Philosophers typically distinguish between *etiological* and *causal-role* senses of 'function'. When employed in its etiological sense, the function of memory would refer to why it was selected for by evolution, whereas in its causal-role sense it would refer to the particular causal contribution it makes for the organism. Etiological and causal-role functional accounts need not contradict each other, of course, but they do call for different evidence. Unfortunately, in the case of memory, both kinds of evidence are tricky. On the one hand, evolutionary evidence is scant and ambiguous, making it hard not to see certain views as mere just-so stories. The idea that memory evolved to track epistemic authority (Mahr & Csibra, 2018), for instance, assumes that there was enough time and evolutionary pressure for such a trait to be that in virtue of which memory was selected for. But why should this be so? Our ancestors presumably had to track all sorts of different things that were critical for survival: predators, dangerous areas, cached food, and so on. Wouldn't it be a more parsimonious account to say that episodic memory evolved to help us keep track of such fitness-enhancing items, and that once there, our ancestors capitalized on an already available tracking system to keep a tally on, among other things, conspecifics' assertions and testimonies? It seems improbable that the fitness-enhancing trait episodic memory evolved for was as phylogenetically recent and culturally dependent as the epistemic authority of our reason-giving practices (De Brigard & Gessell, 2018).

On the other hand, evidence for memory's function in a causal-role sense is also challenging. Successful examples of causal-role functional characterization of biological systems typically require a fairly good understanding of the mechanisms they are embedded in. A causal-role functional characterization of a nephron is possible in part because we know how it is causally structured in the relevant system, that is, the kidney. By contrast, we don't yet have such an understanding of the structural organization of the system episodic memory is supposed to be a part of; indeed, we don't even know how to precisely individuate our episodic memory system or whether it constitutes an independent system at all. True, we may have identified some neural structures that are involved in a number of memory-related tasks, but we are far from understanding the hierarchical structure in which episodic memory is embedded, and therefore from a satisfactory characterization of its causal contribution to the organism. And this relates to a final lesson we can learn from the above discussion: 'function' can also be understood in computational terms. Anderson's model, for instance, is relatively silent about the nature of the mechanisms that instantiate the postulated computations, and yet the research program of rational analysis of memory has been proceeding successfully for years. At the end of the day, we want the etiological, causal-role, and computational accounts of memory's function to be coherent with one another. Until then, though, we ought to be cautious as to what sense of 'function' is being used, what the epistemic reach of the functional explanation is, and what the nature of the evidence it calls for is.

4 What Do We Remember?

Think about your first day of high school and try to recall a particular event on that date. What do you remember? As it turns out, the answer to that question is harder than it seems. One possibility is to say that what you remember is something in the past. But what would that 'thing' be? Is it the objects, persons, or places you interacted with? Or is it rather an event? And, if so, is it the event that transpired externally or do we remember the event of experiencing what transpired externally? Another possibility is to say that what we remember is not a thing in the past but rather something in the present. Recall Aristotle's own concern with the fact that in remembering we are aware of something in the present, not in the past, and thus the answer to what it is that we remember must be something that occurs in the present. A solution is perhaps to say that what we remember is not the event in the past but rather the information contained in a memory trace that we entertain at the time of retrieval. But, if so, what is the nature of such memory traces, how do we know they exist, and how can we find them? These questions have dominated the philosophical discussion about the nature of memory for generations, and thanks to developments in both the philosophy of mind and the science of memory, we have made some progress. To start, let us revisit some useful conceptual distinctions.

4.1 Memory's Object, Content, and Vehicle

Remembering is a mental state and, as such, it is intentional: it is about something. That which a mental state is about is known as its intentional *object*. As Brentano (1874) reminds us, intentional objects need not exist. I can fear the Chupacabra even though – spoiler alert – the Chupacabra does not exist. I can also fear my neighbor's dog, of course, in which case the intentional object of my mental state exists. Nevertheless, to be the intentional object of a mental state, existence is not required. Importantly, intentional objects differ from intentional *contents*. Lois Lane can entertain thoughts about Clark Kent that she does not entertain about Superman. She may think, for instance, "I believe that Clark Kent is a dork and I believe that Superman is not a dork," and yet she wouldn't be contradicting herself, even though both 'Clark Kent' and 'Superman' refer to the same individual: Kal-El. How can this be so? A traditional answer has it that the same intentional object can present to the subject differently, so that each mode of presentation conveys a different content. When Kal-El presents to Lois under the mode of presentation 'Clark Kent', it carries a content that conveys, or at least licenses, the thought that he's a dork. By contrast, when it presents as 'Superman', it carries a different content – one that neither coveys nor licenses the thought that he's a dork.

In contemporary philosophy of mind, there are several approaches to cash out the nature of intentional objects, intentional contents, and the relationship between the two (Rowlands, 2017). Some philosophers hold, for instance, that intentional objects are like any ordinary objects that just happen to not have the property of existence – perhaps just as there are objects that happen to not have the property of being blue or tart – while others hold that they aren't really entities but facts or states-of-affairs that can even obtain counterfactually, and thus can serve as truth-makers of intentional statements about nonexistent entities. Likewise, there are many views on intentional contents. Some philosophers consider contents to be propositional and take propositions to be abstract and mind-independent, whereas others take propositions to be concrete and mind-dependent. Others take contents to be nonpropositional in nature; and finally, there are those who hold mixed approaches, depending on the type of mental state. The project of naturalizing intentionality, as it is often called, is carried out by philosophers who seek to understand how intentional contents can be instantiated in minds like ours, which are not substantially different from the stuff that makes up the rest of the natural world. Among them, in turn, there is a subset of philosophers that take intentional contents to consist in the information carried by representations instantiated in our brains. The inclusive approach I advocate for in this Element favors this general approach to naturalizing mnemonic contents, although it is important to acknowledge that there are nonrepresentational approaches consistent with a naturalistic framework.

Philosophers of mind who take contents to be representations also make a critical distinction between representational *content* and representational *vehicle*. As mentioned, a particular intentional content represents its object in a certain way, but the information that does the representing is different from the particular thing in the world that carries such information. The word 'memory' written in black ink carries the same content if written with sand at the beach or with chocolate frosting on top of a birthday cake, but each token of the word differs in its representational vehicle. The content/vehicle distinction enables us to see that there is a difference between the properties of the content and the properties of its vehicle (Hurley, 1998). One may say, of the word 'memory', that it is evocative regardless of whether it is written in ink, sand, or frosting, but only one of them is yummy. This is because being evocative, say, is a property of the content, while being yummy is a property of the vehicle. The same goes for mental representations, even when taken to be instantiated in the brain. A representationalist who follows the Fodorian tradition of the language of thought may consider that a particular content is carried by a vehicle with certain sentence-like properties, such as discreteness and locality, whereas a partisan of the connectionist tradition may think instead of the vehicle as being distributed and nonlocal. Still, they may agree on the properties of the content itself.

Although a proper treatment of the notions of intentional object, content, and vehicle could easily require its own book, being aware of these distinctions suffices to show that the question of what we remember is ambiguous, as it can call for an answer in terms of the intentional object of a memory, the remembered content, or even the precise vehicle bearing the content retrieved. And, as it happens, philosophers have offered answers to each one of these three versions of the question. Moreover, different views on the nature of memory and of remembering would tend to favor one or another response. For example, if you are a nonrepresentationalist and a direct realist, you may think that the intentional object of a memory is the remembered *thing* itself (Laird, 1920; Woozley, 1949). A behaviorist such as Malcolm (1963) may take the intentional object of a memory to be rather a remembered *event,* and he may even acknowledge that there is some degree of mind-dependency in how events are individuated, in order to account for different ways in which the same event may present to two different witnesses. Another possibility, which is open to both representationalists and nonrepresentationalists, is that the experience of remembering has different intentional objects depending on whether it is veridical or not. A direct realist who is also an externalist about content may argue that the remembered event is constitutive of their memory and, thus, that if there was no such event, the content of the memory would be different from what it would be if the event actually occurred, regardless of whether the memory experience in both cases is indistinguishable. Similarly, a representationalist who is also an internalist about contents can still hold the view that the mental state of a veridical memory whose intentional content represents an event that did obtain is different from that of a non-veridical memory whose intentional content represents one that didn't. Although arguably these *disjunctivist* options are difficult to accommodate with extant empirical evidence, some philosophers have advanced proposals in that direction (Debus, 2008; Schwartz, 2018; Moran, 2021).

Partisans of the epistemic view, by contrast, may consider the intentional objects of a memory to be instead *facts* or *states-of-affairs* expressed by memory beliefs. But, as Fernández (2017) reminds us, understanding the precise nature of the fact expressed by the belief – or, more precisely, the proposition one is related to in a memory belief – is complex, as different memories may refer to different kinds of states-of-affairs. Remembering semantically that Caracas is the capital of Venezuela may have as its intentional object a different state-of-affairs than my episodic memory of remembering learning that Caracas is the capital of Venezuela, even if I learned that Caracas is the capital of Venezuela while I was in Caracas (see Section 2.5). What makes it different? One possibility is to argue that while the states-of-affairs that constitute the intentional object of a semantic memory do not include mental states, the intentional object of episodic memories does, so that when I remember, episodically, my learning that Caracas is the capital of Venezuela, I am talking about a complex state-of-affairs that involves not only the fact expressed by the proposition that Caracas is the capital of Venezuela but also my experience of learning it (Furlong, 1951). More recent approaches have tried to accommodate other distinctive features of episodic memories, such as their self-reference and sense of pastness, by offering even more complex accounts of the propositions expressed by their corresponding memory beliefs and their intentional objects (Fernández, 2017). But now the discussion starts to bleed into the variant of the question "what do we remember?" that arguably has received the most attention in the philosophical literature, namely that about the nature of the representational content of our memories – or, more informally, the nature of memory traces.

4.2 Memory Traces

The notion of memory trace is used by both philosophers and scientists, but it predates the distinction between the two. Plato, as mentioned, references memory traces in the *Theaetetus*, where remembered experiences in memory are compared to seal rings leaving impressions in a wax table. These impressions – the analogy tells us – are representations of the seal ring, just as memory traces are representations of the experiences that created them (*Tht.* 194c–e). Zeno the Stoic and Aristotle also held that experiences leave traces and that such traces give rise to the memories we later retrieve. The idea persisted among classic representationalists and was so widespread that the appeal to memory traces to explain remembering was the received view by the time psychology became an independent discipline at the end of the nineteenth century. Moreover, both philosophers and psychologists agreed that, given the current status of neuroscience, memory traces were merely *hypothetical* (Russell, 1921). Nevertheless, they disagreed as to *how* to interpret the scope of this hypothesis and the way one should go about verifying it. On the one hand, philosophers saw the postulation of memory traces as a *theory-independent hypothesis*. Memory traces were hypothetical precisely because their acceptance within a theory of memory was at stake. From this perspective, the question as to what memory traces are ought to be preceded by a more fundamental question as to whether the notion of memory trace is at all required for a correct account of memory. On the other hand, psychologists thought of memory traces as a *theory-dependent hypothesis*. From their point of view, memory traces were hypothetical not because their postulation needed to be justified but rather because we just didn't know what kind of physical/neural entity they could be (James, 1890). Consequently, while philosophers (e.g., Russell, 1921) took the hypothetical status of memory traces to be settled primarily at a conceptual level, psychologists thought of the task as an empirical one: one of finding out the nature and precise location of memory traces – or 'engrams' (Semon, 1904/1921) – in the brain.

To be fair, not all psychologists and neuroscientists accepted the existence of memory traces in the first half of the twentieth century. Behaviorists notoriously jettisoned most talk of them, and the idea that we could dispense of the term altogether was seen as vindicated by Karl Lashley – who trained under the behaviorist J. B. Watson – when he published his famous paper "In Search of the Engram," in which he declared that "it is not possible to demonstrate the isolated localization of a memory trace anywhere within the nervous system" (Lashley, 1950: 481). Although, in my opinion, Lashley's article should be read as supporting an epistemic claim about the limits of our methods to identify memory traces, the fact remains that many interpreted it as providing conclusive evidence for an ontological thesis against their existence.

Nevertheless, by the mid-century, two relatively contemporaneous discoveries resurrected the scientific hope of finding memory traces in the brain. The first one was the case of H. M., whose selective memory impairment strikingly opposed Lashley's views, for it showed that there was a clear dissociation between a brain area – the hippocampus – that was required for the creation of new memories and the retention of recent ones and brain areas that were not. The second discovery took a bit longer but was equally influential. Work in synaptic plasticity in hippocampal cells led neurophysiologists to rapidly stimulate (i.e., 'tetanic' stimulation) the presynaptic membrane to increase the speed and the repetition of electrical activity, which in turn allowed them to extend the life of the electrical signal they were recording in the postsynaptic cell. Researchers in Per Andersen's neurophysiology lab in Oslo began to observe what appeared to be a correlation between the frequency and duration of the tetanic burst in the presynaptic cell and the length and enhancement of the postsynaptic response, ranging from a few seconds up to about ten minutes. This experimental trick soon became an object of research in and of itself, as researchers began to wonder about the underlying mechanisms that allowed hippocampal cells to retain their synaptic potentiation long after the electric stimulus was removed. The first description of the underlying mechanism of this phenomenon, known now as long-term potentiation (or LTP), was offered by Bliss and Lomo in 1973 (Craver, 2003). The discovery of a neural mechanism that could preserve the effects of a stimulus once removed, and the fact that such mechanism happened to be found in a region that was demonstrably necessary for the formation of new memories, gave a new life to the scientific research on memory traces (Josselyn et al., 2015).

4.2.1 Do Memory Traces Exist?

These impressive findings notwithstanding, the philosopher may remain skeptical, for the underlying question as to whether we are justified in postulating the existence of memory traces has yet to receive a satisfactory answer. The reason, as Russell (1921: lecture IV) reminds us, is that the notion of memory trace or "engram [... is] in fact, hypothetical, invoked for theoretical uses, and not an outcome of direct observation." Indeed, neither the case of H. M. nor the discovery of LTP provides observational evidence for the existence of memory traces; at most, they show us that there is a particular brain region needed to perform some mnemonic tasks or that certain molecular mechanisms prolong a neuronal process thought to underlie some kinds of learning. Even today, 'memory traces' feature in our accounts of remembering as theoretical terms referring to yet unobserved – maybe even unobservable – entities whose existence is postulated via inference to the best explanation. The worry, though, is that, as with many other theoretical notions that are so introduced, their need depends on there not being an equally good – or even better – explanation which does not invoke them. 'Phlogiston' was introduced as a theoretical term to refer to a hypothetical entity supposedly released during combustion. Once there was an account that could equally fit the observable data without the need for postulating phlogiston, the term was abandoned and the status of phlogiston as a real entity was denied. But other theoretical terms, such as 'electron', were also introduced for theoretical purposes, and now their putative referents live happily among the existing. So, we may ask, is 'memory trace' akin to 'phlogiston' or is it rather like 'electron'?

According to the standard view, the term 'memory trace' was introduced in reference to an unobservable entity or process, M, thought to exist during a period of time, t_2, between a time, t_1, in which a subject, S, experiences an event x, Ex, and a subsequent time, t_3, in which S remembers x, Rx. Additionally, for a particular M to be a memory trace – as opposed to some other enabling process – it was assumed that three conditions must obtain:

(1) S's M must have been caused by Ex at t_1 and it must in turn cause Rx at t_3 (*causal condition*)
(2) S's M must retain through t_2 the same intentional content entertained during Ex at t_1 and later retrieved at t_3 during Rx (*retention condition*)
(3) S's M must preserve structure of intentional object x in the intentional content retained during t_2 from Ex to Rx (*isomorphism condition*).

The existence of memory traces is thought to help to explain the facts that the remembered event and its recollection are temporally distant, that the intentional content retrieved is the same as that of the original experience, and that such content in turn corresponds to its intentional object – that is, the actual event.

A first wave of skepticism about memory traces was fueled by Russell's positivist adherence to verificationism: to make scientific claims about memory and remembering meaningful, we were advised not to appeal to unobservable – and, thus, unverifiable – causal intermediaries. Instead, Russell proposed the notion of 'mnemic causation', whereby the past experience directly causes the subsequent recollection. A similar anti-realism about memory traces was present in Wittgenstein (1953), Ryle (1949), Benjamin (1956), and, more judiciously articulated, in Malcom (1963: 237), who forcefully asserted that "our use of the language of memory" carries no implication about the causes of our remembering or about the causal mechanisms involved in our recollections. We can perfectly grasp the concepts of memory and remembering without any reference whatsoever to the cause of that which is remembered, and much less to a causal link between the past experience and its subsequent recollection (see Section 3.2.2).

Malcolm's anti-realist stance was quickly countered by Martin and Deutscher (1963). The main purpose of that paper, as you may recall, was to argue for the claim that a causal condition is required for a proper analysis of our concept of remembering. Some of their arguments are based on cases in which individuals have a particular Ex at t_1, then forget it during t_2, and then at t_3 do something "for which the only reasonable explanation" is that they experienced x at t_1. More precisely, Martin and Deutscher's strategy was to argue for the necessity of the causal condition abductively, via an inference to the best explanation. To illustrate, consider again the variation on the painter's case from Section 3.3.2. Having been asked to draw an image of a car by a 'stop' sign, and having produced an image identical to that in the lefthand panel of Figure 3, the inference we are invited to draw – that is, the inference that best explains your behavior – is that you are actually drawing that image from memory, not from imagination, and that you simply had forgotten seeing it before. Moreover, Martin and Deutscher thought that the existence of memory traces followed from the acceptance of a causal condition, since denying their reality would commit us to Ex diachronically causing Rx, and they thought that causation at a temporal distance was metaphysically unpalatable. The appeal to memory traces was then the result of an inference to the best explanation: they were postulated to help explain the causal connection between Ex and Rx without having to accept a metaphysically questionable causal process (De Brigard, 2020).

Malcolm was unconvinced, though, and a few years later argued anew against memory traces by claiming that, even if one accepts Martin and Deutscher's arguments for a causal condition, we can still reject the need to postulate their existence. His argument, reminiscent of Russell's defense of mnemic causation, is that the kind of explanation we usually invoke when talking about remembering does not involve any reference to a process or entity mediating Ex and Rx. Suppose that you experience a certain event, you tell it to someone, and for some reason they do not believe you: "How do you know that you remember it?," they may ask, to which you reply: "Because I saw it happen!" That "because" is causal alright, just as Martin and Deutscher suggested, but there is no further need to make a reference to any kind of causal entity or process mediating the event experienced and its recollection: "We can agree with Martin and Deutscher that the language of memory does, in a sense, require a 'causal interpretation,' but not agree that memory as a causal concept entails the concept of causal process. ... Eliminate the assumption of a causal process, and the causal argument for a memory trace collapses" (Malcolm, 1977: 185). Indeed, causal explanations involving action at a temporal distance are, according to Malcolm, perfectly suitable to explain recollection, and nothing about intermediate causal processes is implied by our use of the concept of remembering. In sum, while we can agree that a causal condition is needed to explain how *Ex* causes *Rx*, we need not accept the additional inference to the best explanation in which memory traces are postulated.

Although the dialectic between realist and anti-realists about memory traces has largely been the result of arguments involving the causal condition (1), other philosophers have argued against memory traces by criticizing the retention (2) and the isomorphism (3) conditions. Some claim, for instance, that it makes little sense to speak of an entity as retaining or preserving content unchanged through time (Squires, 1969) or that they need to do so in a format that is structurally isomorphic to the remembered experience or event (Rosen, 1975). Others argued that memory traces cannot meet the isomorphism condition because experiences are unstructured, so there is no structure to preserve and retrieve (Heil, 1978), or because memory traces should not be thought of as individual and discrete bearers of mnemonic content – as opposed to distributed representations with overlapping information, as suggested by connectionist approaches to mental representation (Sutton, 1998). Moreover, as Robins (2016) warns us, if we were to accept a distributed notion of memory trace, the causal view would be compromised, as such a conception of mnemonic representation lacks the resources to relate a discrete neural structure to a particular experienced event, as it is demanded by the causal view. Finally, some argue that memory traces need not preserve exactly the same content from *Ex* to *Rx* and instead support the view that retrieved contents may include information not explicitly represented at encoding (Michaelian, 2011).

Despite these criticisms, eliminating the notion of 'memory trace' from our accounts of memory and remembering may not be so easy, as there are instances of memory-related phenomena for which an appeal to memory traces still constitutes a better explanation than an alternative one in which memory traces are not postulated. As De Brigard (2020) argued, the examples employed by anti-realists about memory traces only involve successful recollection.

However, when it comes to explaining instances of unsuccessful recollection, cases involving between-subject differences at retrieval, or even differences due to interventions between encoding at t_1 and retrieval at t_3, a reference to an intermediate causal mechanism between Ex and Rx becomes indispensable. Another memory-related phenomenon difficult to account for without reference to a memory trace involves content-specific deletions during memory reactivation and reconsolidation. Recall that, according to the traditional encoding–storage–retrieval model of remembering, once a memory is consolidated and stored, it remains unalterable. However, in the past couple of decades, research has demonstrated that, when a memory is reactivated, it is labile and prone to modification for a short period of time, after which it is once again stable and stored (Hardt et al., 2010). Manipulations conducted during this 'reconsolidation' period, using both behavioral and pharmacological interventions, show content-specific changes that affect memories for unique events. For instance, evidence suggests that administering propranolol, a synthetic beta-adrenergic receptor blocker, immediately after memory reactivation, disrupts the reconsolidation of stimulus-specific fear-conditioning responses, effectively acting as an amnestic agent (Dębiec & LeDoux, 2004). It would be challenging to explain these observations without appealing to intermediary memory traces whose contents are somehow altered during retrieval.

So, memory traces may not go the way of phlogiston, but does that mean that we need to accept their existence? Not necessarily. Here, the philosophy of memory can take a page from the philosophy of science, where scientific anti-realists (e.g., van Fraassen, 1980) admonish that inference to the best explanation is always relative to the set of available explanations, a set that could include only false ones, and thus the leap from being a theoretical term that is explanatorily indispensable to the ontological conclusion that its putative referent exists is unwarranted. Appealing to memory traces in explanatory contexts may constitute the best alternative available to us – as opposed to the best alternative *tout court* – in order to account for several memory-related phenomena, but to be able to conclude that they exist, we need more than an inference to the best explanation. We may need more conclusive, perhaps even observational evidence, before we can count memory traces in our ontology. Yet, to be able to know what to look for, we may need to know first what they are.

4.2.2 What Are Memory Traces?

Uncertainty about their existence hasn't prevented philosophers from speculating about the nature of memory traces. Indeed, most representationalists about remembering tend to favor some particular view on the nature of memory traces,[10] with differences among views stemming from, first, the fact that not all representationalists adhere to conditions (1) to (3) and, second, the fact that each condition leaves some room for interpretation. To help to chart the logical space for different varieties of memory traces, it is helpful to consider first a major distinction based on the relationship between the perceived and the remembered content (De Brigard, 2014a; Michaelian & Sutton, 2017). On the one hand, those who adhere to conditions (1) to (3) tend to be content *invariantists*, holding that the content of the memory trace is the same as both the perceived content during encoding and the remembered content during retrieval. On the other hand, content *variantists*, who do not adhere to one or more of the conditions (1) to (3), deny that the content of the memory trace is the same as either the perceived and/or the remembered content. In turn, there are different flavors of content invariantism/variatism based on how you think mnemonic contents relate to both perceived and remembered contents. For instance, one can take perception to be nonrepresentational (i.e., direct), so the content of a memory trace is only created at t_2, after encoding, and then reactivated at t_3, unchanged, during retrieval. This version of invariantism is called *direct invariantism*. Its counterpart, *direct variantism*, takes the change in retrieved content to occur between the stored content in t_2 and the retrieved one in t_3. *Indirect invariantism*, by contrast, takes perception to be representational, so that the perceptual content at t_1 is the same content stored during t_2 and then retrieved at t_3. Its counterpart, *indirect variantism*, offers three opportunities for content change: (a) between t_1 and t_2, so the perceived content is different from the stored and retrieved one; (b) between t_2 and t_3, so the perceived content is the same as the stored content but different from the retrieved one; or (c) between t_1 and t_2 and between t_2 and t_3, so the perceived, stored, and retrieved contents are different. Finally, *non-retentional invariantism* – which rejects condition (2) – has it that the remembered content at t_3 is identical to the perceptual content at t_1, but not in virtue of there being any content being retained through t_2. Its counterpart, *non-retentional variantism*, holds then that the contents at t_1 and t_3 differ, just as they do from the content of the memory trace stored during t_2.[11]

In practice, most contemporary representationalists hold some version of content variantism – which is surprising, given that the received view of

---

[10] Note that not all representationalists think of memory traces as neural entities. One could be a dualist and a representationalist and hold that memory traces are mental rather than physical.

[11] Prima facie, this view would seem at odds with the need to postulate memory traces. What would be their use if the retrieved content is different from both the encoded and the stored contents? The answer, as I will discuss in a second, is that memory traces help to solve not only a question about a diachronic content–content relation but also a diachronic cause–effect relation, and someone may still want to hold on to the causal efficacy of the memory trace qua representational vehicle even if they deny the need for a retained representational content.

memory traces postulates (2) as a necessary condition. What could explain this striking conflict? One possibility is that philosophers may take the differences in the conscious experience of *Ex* during t_1 and the conscious experience of *Rx* during t_3 as being accidental or nonessential to their mnemonic content. Stout (1899: 435), for instance, when arguing that memory is essentially reproductive, states that to remember is to reinstate the objects of past experiences "in the order and manner of their original occurrence," suggesting that what is essential to the content is the spatiotemporal structure of what is remembered, rather than its phenomenology. A problem with this view is that many common changes from encoding to retrieval involve differences in the spatiotemporal structure of the remembered content. For instance, sometimes the egocentric perspective from which an event was experienced gets allocentrically encoded instead, leading us to remember it from a different point of view (McCarroll, 2018). Spatial and temporal distortions are common too, with people frequently experiencing childhood spaces as being smaller than remembered or past events as being more recent than they were – a phenomenon known as the "telescoping effect" (Jansen et al., 2006). Another possibility is that philosophers hold (2) because they think about intentional contents as propositions. If propositions are eternal, unchanging, and imperishable, then it isn't shocking that one may hold that the content *Ex* at t_1 can be preserved in *M* through t_2 and be numerically and qualitatively identical to *Rx* at *t3*. As such, perhaps only partisans of the epistemic view and/or representationalists that take mental contents to be extramental entities would be truly invariantists. Treating contents as extra-mental propositions, however, opens up more questions than it answers and helps little to understand the nature of memory traces. Thankfully, most inclusive philosophers of memory take intentional contents to be part of the natural world and recognize that remembered contents tend to be different from the contents of the original experiences.

Philosophers differ, though, in how to characterize the nature of the variation from *Ex* to *Rx*. Some take the changes to be *subtractive*: relative to perceptions, for instance, memories are said to be less forceful (Hobbes, 1651/1994) or vivid (Hume, 1739/1978). Others take these changes to be *additive*: in addition to the original – albeit fainter – content, an accompanying 'memory marker' is thought to be attached. For some, the memory marker was *cognitive*: an annexed thought about the duration of the past perception (Spinoza, 1677/1992: 83) or a thought that one has had such a perception before (Locke, 1694/1979). Others thought of the additional mental state as *affective*: a feeling of pastness, a kind of conscious awareness of having had the experience before (James, 1890), or even a feeling of familiarity associated with the belief that one experienced the event in the past (Russell, 1921). Finally, some philosophers thought of memory markers closer to a second-order representation or *apperception* (Leibniz, 1714/ 1989), suggesting that perhaps only organisms capable of self-reflection can have episodic memories. Moreover, given the different versions of variantism, there are several possibilities to account for subtractive and additive changes. One may argue, for instance, that the encoded content loses vivacity from t_1 to t_2 and acquires a feeling of familiarity from t_2 to t_3. In sum, most philosophers who adhere to some version of representationalism accept that the remembered content differs in important respects from the content entertained during the original experience. Nevertheless, representationalists can easily adhere to the received view of memory traces by modifying condition (2), via the stipulation that the retained content retrieved at t_3 during Rx should be both accurate and sufficiently similar to the content entertained during Ex at t_1 (Bernecker, 2010). How to make these accuracy and similarity conditions precise enough is, however, a matter of contention.

Disagreement also abounds when it comes to understanding how the contents of memory traces are represented, that is, what the nature of their representational vehicles are. Except for advocates of the extended cognition hypothesis (e.g., Clark & Chalmers, 1998), most contemporary representationalists take memory traces to be some sort of brain entity. One view takes them to be *localized* representations, that is, discrete symbolic entities individually coding for specific events. Localizationist views, alas, have a hard time accommodating many mnemonic phenomena, such as the fact that damage to selective cortical regions produces uneven patterns of forgetting or the fact that one can access stored information more or less successfully via distinct retrieval strategies (but see Gallistel, 2010). *Connectionist* models offered many advantages over localizationist ones when it comes to explaining such phenomena (e.g., graceful degradation, assignation by omission) by postulating that mnemonic contents are distributed, by way of being encoded in the connection weights between neuronal units (Rumerhart et al., 1986). A *hybrid* possibility is to think of memory traces of complex events as being distributed, insofar that each requires the engagement of multiple units, but with each neuron encoding basic local information within them, likely in molecular structures (Gershman, 2022).

Finally, another dimension along which views on memory traces vary corresponds to the degree of explicitness of the represented content. Some may hold that while the represented content in M is a stripped-down version of that encoded during Ex, it is still *explicitly* encoded in the brain – suggesting that, were we to develop the technology to identify them, we could directly read them off neural structures. Others claim, instead, that contents are only *implicitly* encoded, and that an additional process – that is, retrieval – is needed to make them explicit. Lastly, there are some that argue that contents are not occurrent – and thus are neither explicitly nor implicitly encoded – but rather *dispositional*, that is, what gets encoded is a disposition to revive a content at retrieval given the right cue. Unsurprisingly, all these views face criticisms. Explicit accounts of mnemonic contents, for instance, inherit all the difficulties of trying to naturalize intentional contents in the brain (Hutto, 2021), whereas implicit and dispositional accounts of content inherit the difficulties pointed out by earlier discussions on tacit knowledge, such as the fact that at any time we may implicitly be representing infinitively many contents or the fact that their referents could be massively disjunctive (Vosgerau, 2010). In short, sundry philosophical theories about the nature of memory traces differ along many dimensions, and the debate about their viability is current and lively, so a fair coverage of them all could require a separate work on its own. Thus, instead, I will finish this section by briefly offering a scientifically grounded account of memory traces that seeks to reconcile the need for postulating intermediate causal mechanisms from *Ex* to *Rx* while also supporting the simulationist claim that remembering is, essentially, reconstructive.

4.3 Memory Traces and Simulationism

The account I have in mind builds upon the influential hippocampal indexing theory (HIT). Initially proposed by Teyler and DiScena (1986), HIT sought to explain the nature of the memory traces formed during the encoding of an episode and later retrieved during recollection. Consistent with the SMM (see Section 2.5) and the complementary learning systems model (McClelland et al., 1995), HIT postulates that, when an event is experienced, two kinds of consolidation occur: first, there is a rapid, *cellular* consolidation in which information is encoded as connectivity changes among the neurons involved in processing the encoded event. With time, a second, *systems* consolidation takes place, whereby the connections between the relevant hippocampal-neocortical regions are further strengthened (Figure 4).[12] To illustrate, consider how the model would explain the formation a memory trace of, say, the actual event (not the photos) depicted in the left panel of Figure 3. You are walking down the street and see a car failing to stop at a 'stop' sign, knocking down a pedestrian. This experience involves the

---

[12] As mentioned, the SMM initially postulated that, once consolidated, the hippocampus was no longer needed for retrieval. However, a careful examination of extant data now clearly indicates that the hippocampus is still required for the retrieval of both recent and remote memories and that the degree of preserved memories in individuals with hippocampal amnesia is proportional to the amount of hippocampal tissue preserved (Nadel & Moscovitch, 1997). Thus, HIT is consistent with this further development in the science of memory.

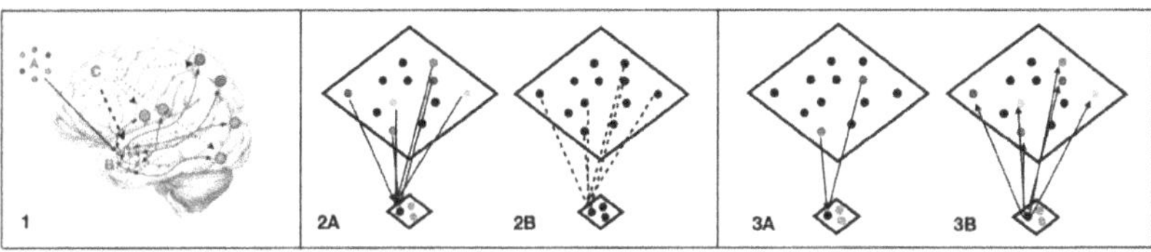

Figure 4 Hippocampal indexing theory (HIT).

Note: (1) *Graphical schematic in brain space.* An initial stimulus with multiple sensory properties is first experienced (A). A rapid consolidation occurs in the hippocampus (B) while the sensory information of the stimulus is processed in the relevant regions of the cortex. This coactivation creates an association between the sensory regions and a hippocampal index. At retrieval, a top-down signal from the prefrontal cortex to elements of the hippocampal-cortical assembly reactivates the network and, thus, the memory content. (2) *Encoding.* The bigger layer indicates units in the neocortex, with different colors indicating different sensory information. The smaller layer indicates specific synaptic activity uniquely associated with the pattern of neocortical activation (2A). After encoding, consolidation strengthens the connection between the hippocampal index and the associated neurons in the neocortex (2B). (3) *Retrieval.* A cue can reactivate a subset of the neocortical pattern, which in turn reactivates the hippocampal index (3A). This reactivation further spreads to the rest of the hippocampal-neocortical network, effectively reinstating the encoded pattern (3B).

activation of several cortical regions: the auditory cortex processes the sounds, the visual cortex processes the shapes and colors of the objects, lateral temporal cortices help to categorize them, and so on. An active hippocampus helps to bind this information together in a large hippocampal-neocortical network which, in time, becomes systems-consolidated. A day later, you are summoned as a witness to recall the event and are asked if you remember the car failing to stop at a 'stop' sign. This auditory cue helps to re-activate a subset of the encoded neuronal pattern – maybe some visual or semantic information pertaining to the sign – which in turn propagates to a hippocampal *index* further re-activating the rest of the neuronal pattern, effectively reinstating the encoded hippocampal-neocortical network.[13] Given that the vehicle of the encoded representation is reactivated, then the encoded content is reenacted and, thus, you manage to remember the event.

The framework offered by HIT affords several advantages for the empirically minded simulationist who is uncomfortable with the idea of giving up memory traces. According to this view, when entertaining the intentional content of an

---

[13] The nature of this index is controversial. In its original formulation, this index was considered as a "simple memory" (Marr, 1974), a kind of sketchy or abstract representation of the whole event. But others disagree. Fleshing out the nature of this index is critical but beyond the scope of this Element. However, I try to do so in De Brigard (in press).

experienced event *Ex* at t_1, a particular representational vehicle is formed, that is, a certain hippocampal-neocortical network in the brain. Consolidation strengthens the propensity of different units of the network to coactivate given the right cue. During t_2, when the memory is not retrieved, the individual units of the encoded network are constantly deployed for their regular cognitive purposes. However, when a relevant cue is presented in a retrieval context, the activation among connected units is propagated and thus the hippocampal-neocortical network is reactivated, reinstating the intentional content *Rx* at t_3. A memory trace, *M*, is, on this account, the dispositional property of a neural network to reinstate the state it was in, during encoding, at the time of retrieval. By characterizing it as a dispositional property of the vehicle rather than the content, we avoid the abovementioned concerns about content dispositionalism (Vosgerau, 2010). Also, by treating *M* as a dispositional property, we can readily explain why unexpected cues can bring about involuntary memories. Moreover, this account can help to explain why, when a memory is reactivated, it becomes malleable and modifiable. After all, every act of retrieval is itself an act of re-encoding, and thus the pattern of activation can vary more or less drastically, contaminating the information from the initial episode with details acquired during its retrieval, reconsolidation and further re-indexing by the hippocampus (Hardt et al., 2010). Incidentally, the view also accommodates the fact that information acquired during t_2, and unrelated to the encoded event at t_1, might nonetheless affect the way we remember it at *t3*. Here's an example. Long ago, when I did not know English, I learned the chorus to "A Hard Day's Night" by the Beatles. I did not know what it meant, but I could sing the words. Years later, after learning English, I found myself listening to the song again and was able to remember the lyrics to sing along. But now, as I was remembering the words, I was also understanding them for the very first time. The content of my recollection was different from that of its encoding, due to an intervening change to the network units that formed the representational vehicle of my memory.

Importantly, thinking about memory traces in this way can help to accommodate the two main motivations for the simulation view of remembering. First, the systematicity of ordinary false episodic memories can be seen as a natural fallout of the pattern completion process that occurs at retrieval. In practice, encoding is never infallible, and many of the connections between units engaged during *Ex* are likely not strengthened during consolidation, so the reactivated hippocampal-neocortical network is typically incomplete. Thankfully, due to statistical regularities in the connections of such units, the probability of reactivating the right set of connections tends to be high. This is the sense in which retrieval can be said to be both probabilistically reconstructed and veridical. However, since units in the hippocampal-neocortical network have themselves additional existing associations with numerous other units, it is possible that a unit or a set of units not involved in *Ex* can become active during pattern completion at retrieval, resulting in a *Rx* that does not accurately represent the event represented by *Ex*.

There is plenty of research trying to understand the precise computations that best describe the mechanisms of pattern formation – or 'separation' – and pattern completion at retrieval. A promising avenue, in my view, is to think of these computations along the lines of Anderson's rational analysis model (Section 3.4), whereby extant associations can influence the pattern of neural activation by combining values reflecting prior frequencies as well as previously acquired conceptual associations. Thus, you can explain the example in which you falsely recall having seen a 'stop' sign when you actually saw a 'yield' sign by arguing that the process of pattern completion that took place at retrieval – upon being asked if you have seen the car stop at a 'stop' sign – involved a probabilistic assignment of the part of the content representing the traffic sign that was biased by a strong association between the cue word (i.e., 'stop sign') and a mental representation of a 'stop' sign as well as a prior frequency of having experienced many 'stop' signs in similar street corners.

Second, the proposed model can also shed light on the reason behind the neural and cognitive commonalities between episodic memory and other varieties of episodic simulation, such as episodic future and counterfactual thinking. The role of the hippocampal index in the neural network bearing a mnemonic content has been characterized in terms of its capacity to bind together disaggregated components of an episode into a single coherent spatiotemporal scene. The index per se need not represent the information processed in the neocortex but it enables such information to be incorporated into a spatiotemporal scene that can mentally unfold in our consciousness over time (De Brigard, in press). Since a working hippocampus is required to generate similar spatiotemporally structured mental simulations, then we should expect to see difficulties in the spatiotemporal structure and coherence of episodic simulations in individuals with MTL damage as well as impoverished content-wise simulations in individuals with damage to the sensory cortex but preserved hippocampus. This is exactly what the evidence suggests (e.g., De Brigard & Gessell, 2016). Moreover, when future or counterfactual thoughts do not involve the spatiotemporal structuring we associate with episodic memory, but rather less imagistic and more conceptual and/or linguistic processing, we shouldn't expect to see a similar neural architecture as that required for episodic recollection. Again, the evidence supports this prediction as well (e.g., De Brigard & Parikh, 2019). In sum, similar hippocampal-neocortical assemblies are recruited during certain kinds of episodic simulations because the computations that underlie their generation are not that dissimilar from those involved in episodic recollection.

Although there is plenty more to say about the current scientific understanding of memory traces in general, and about the probabilistic-dispositional account I favor, I hope that what I have said so far allows us to see how we can dissolve the conflict between causalist and simulationist theories of remembering. In its strongest form, causalism requires the exact same content Ex encoded at t_1 to be explicitly represented in M and preserved through t_2 all the way to its being retrieved during Rx at t_3. But our preceding discussion makes clear that nobody believes such a strong claim anymore; most – if not all – representationalists are content variantists. But that does not mean that by accepting variantism, even in the radical constructivist form defended by simulationists, we must jettison memory traces. Recall that memory traces were introduced as theoretical posits to explain both a causal connection between encoding at t_1 and retrieval at t_3 and the relationship between the intentional contents of Ex and Rx. Thinking of M as a dispositional property of a representational *vehicle* acquired at t_1 and actualized during retrieval at t_3 allows us to understand why Ex was entertained during encoding and Rx during retrieval *and* why the latter causally depends on the former. Reconsidering the nature of memory traces in light of current cognitive psychology and neuroscience could help dissolve the philosophical debate between the causal and the simulation views of remembering (for related views, see Vosgerau, 2010; Perrin, 2018; Werning, 2020).

5 Final Thoughts

Memory has played a fundamental role in many aspects of philosophy. For many, it constitutes the foundation of our personal identity through time. Others have argued that truth preservation in deductive reasoning depends on a reliable memory. And many, too, have linked memory to issues of responsibility, blameworthiness, and punishment. The role of memory in each of these debates could easily require a separate work. Yet, despite its importance, memory was a somewhat neglected topic in philosophy of mind until relatively recently. As a result, I chose to focus this introductory Element on three foundational issues, mentioned as early as in Aristotle's *De memoria*, which have received quite a bit of attention from philosophers of memory in the last couple of decades: the nature of the faculty of memory, the nature of remembering, and the nature of memory representations.

Moreover, in the spirit of what I have called the "inclusive approach to philosophy," I have brought to bear phenomenological, conceptual, and empirical evidence on an equal footing. Yet by no means do I think that any of these pieces of evidence should be accepted unquestionably. On the contrary, if there is one thing we can learn from different developments in the philosophy of memory it is that many assumptions in the science of memory are rather questionable. Scientists who disagree on the nature of memory traces, for instance, may ultimately have different views as to whether they are tackling them as representational contents or representational vehicles (Robins, 2020). Likewise, those that take remembering and imagining to be distinct from one another may not be clear as to whether they are talking about the processes of remembering and imagining or the faculties of memory and imagination (De Brigard, 2017). Finally, philosophers of memory should also be open to revising conceptual conclusions in light of empirical or phenomenological counterevidence. Both the philosophy and the science of memory have much to contribute to each other when it comes to understanding the nature of memory and remembering.

References

Addis, D. R., Wong, A. T., & Schacter, D. L. (2007). Remembering the past and imagining the future: Common and distinct neural substrates during event construction and elaboration. *Neuropsychologia*, 45(7): 1363–1377.

Anderson, J. R. (1990). *The Adaptive Character of Thought*. Hillsdale, NJ: Lawrence Erlbaum.

Anderson, J. R. & Milson, R. (1989). Human memory: An adaptive perspective. *Psychological Review*, 96: 703–719.

Anderson, M. (2015). *After Phrenology*. Cambridge, MA: MIT Press.

Aronowitz, S. (2023). Semanticization challenges the episodic-semantic distinction. *British Journal for the Philosophy of Science*.

Atance, C. M. & O'Neill, D. K. (2002). Episodic future thinking. *Trends in Cognitive Sciences*, 5(12): 533–539 https://doi.org/10.1086/721760.

Augustin. (2006). *Confessions*. Harmondsworth: Penguin.

Ayer, A. J. (1956). *The Problem of Knowledge*. Cambridge, MA: Hackett.

Benjamin, B. S. (1956). Remembering. *Mind*, 65(259): 312–331.

Bergson, H. (1896/1908). *Matter and Memory*. New York: Zone Books.

Bernecker, S. (2010). *Memory*. Oxford: Oxford University Press.

Bernecker, S. (2017). A causal theory of mnemonic confabulation. *Frontiers in Psychology*, 8: 1207.

Bliss, T. V. & Lømo, T. (1973). Long-lasting potentiation of synaptic transmission in the dentate area of the anaesthetized rabbit following stimulation of the perforant path. *Journal of Physiology*, 232(2): 331–356.

Borges, J. L. (1944). *Ficciones*. Buenos Aires: Editorial Sur.

Boyle, A. (2022). The mnemonic functions of episodic memory. *Philosophical Psychology*, 35(3): 327–349.

Brentano, F. (1874). *Psychologie vom empirischen Standpunkte*. Leipzig: Duncker & Humblot.

Brewer, W. F. & Treyens, J. C. (1981). Role of schemata in memory for places. *Cognitive Psychology*, 13(2): 207–230.

Carr, D. (1979). The logic of knowing how and ability. *Mind*, 88(351): 394–409.

Clark, A. & Chalmers, D. (1998). The extended mind. *Analysis*, 58(1): 7–19.

Cohen, N. & Squire, L. R. (1980). Preserved learning and retention of pattern analyzing skill in amnesia: Dissociation of knowing how and knowing that. *Science*, 210: 207–209.

Copenhaver, R. (2017). John Locke and Thomas Reid. In S. Bernecker & K. Michaelian (Eds.), *The Routledge Handbook of Philosophy of Memory* (pp. 470–479). Abingdon: Routledge.

Corkin, S. (1968). Acquisition of motor skill after bilateral medial temporal-lobe excision. *Neuropsychologia*, 6: 255–265.

Corkin, S. (1984). Lasting consequences of bilateral medial temporal lobectomy: Clinical course and experimental findings in H. M. *Seminars in Neurology*, 4(2): 249–259.

Corkin, S. (2013). *Permanent Present Tense: The Unforgettable Life of the Amnesic Patient H. M.* New York: Basic Books.

Craver, C. (2003). The making of a memory mechanism. *Journal of the History of Biology*, 36: 153–195.

Crystal, J. D. & Glanzman, D. L. (2013). A biological perspective on memory. *Current Biology*, 23(17): R728–R731.

Dębiec, J. & LeDoux, J. E. (2004). Disruption of reconsolidation but not consolidation of auditory fear conditioning by noradrenergic blockade in the amygdala. *Neuroscience*, 129(2): 267–272.

De Brigard, F. (2014a). The nature of memory traces. *Philosophy Compass*, 9 (6): 402–414.

De Brigard, F. (2014b). Is memory for remembering? Recollection as a form of episodic hypothetical thinking. *Synthese*, 191(2): 155–185.

De Brigard, F. (2017). Memory and imagination. In S. Bernecker & K. Michaelian (Eds.), *The Routledge Handbook of Philosophy of Memory* (pp. 127–140). Abingdon: Routledge.

De Brigard, F. (2019). Know-how, intellectualism, and memory systems. *Philosophical Psychology*, 32(5): 720–759.

De Brigard, F. (2020). The explanatory indispensability of memory traces. *The Harvard Review of Philosophy*, 27: 23–47.

De Brigard, F. (in press). Simulationism and memory traces. In S. Aronowitz & L. Nadel (Eds.), *Memory, Space and Time*. Oxford: Oxford University Press.

De Brigard, F., Addis, D., Ford, J. H., Schacter, D. L., & Giovanello, K. S. (2013). Remembering what could have happened: Neural correlates of episodic counterfactual thinking. *Neuropsychologia*, 51(12): 2401–2414.

De Brigard, F. & Gessell, B. S. (2016). Time is not of the essence: Understanding the neural correlates of mental time travel. In K. Michaelian, S. B. Klein, & K. K. Szpunar (Eds.), *Seeing the Future: Theoretical Perspectives on Future-Oriented Mental Time Travel* (pp. 153–179). New York: Oxford University Press.

De Brigard, F. & Gessell, B. S. (2018). Why episodic memory may not be for communication. *Behavioral and Brain Sciences*, 41: e8, https://doi.org/10.1017/S0140525X17001303.

De Brigard, F. & Parikh, N. (2019). Episodic counterfactual thinking. *Current Directions in Psychological Science*, 28(1): 59–66.

De Brigard, F., Umanath, S., & Irish, M. (2022). Rethinking the distinction between episodic and semantic memory: Insights from the past, present and future. *Memory and Cognition*, 50: 459–463.

Debus, D. (2008). Experiencing the past: A relational account of recollective memory. *dialectica*, 62(4): 405–432.

Debus, D. (2010). Accounting for epistemic relevance: A new problem for the causal theory of memory. *American Philosophical Quarterly*, 47(1): 17–29.

Debus, D. (2014). "Mental time travel": Remembering the past, imagining the future, and the particularity of events. *Review of Philosophy and Psychology*, 5: 333–350.

Descartes, R. (1649/1985). The passions of the soul. In J. Cottingham, R. Stoothoff, & D. Murdoch (Eds.), *The Philosophical Writings of Descartes* (pp. 325–404). Cambridge: Cambridge University Press.

Descartes, R. (1991). *The Philosophical Writings of Descartes*, Vol. 3. Cambridge: Cambridge University Press.

Dew, I. T. Z. & Cabeza, R. (2011). The porous boundaries between explicit and implicit memory: Behavioral and neural evidence. *Annals of the New York Academy of Sciences* 1224: 174–190.

Dokic, J. (2014). Feeling the past: A two-tiered account of episodic memory. *Review of Philosophy and Psychology*, 5(3): 413–426.

Dranseika, V. (2020). False memories and quasi-memories. *Oxford Studies in Experimental Philosophy*, 3(3): 175–188.

Dudai, Y. (2007). Memory: It's all about representations. In H. L. Roediger III, Y. Dudai, & S. M. Fitzpatrick (Eds.), *Science of Memory: Concepts* (pp. 13–16). Oxford: Oxford University Press.

Eberhard, D. M., Simons, G. F., & Fennig, C. D. (2022). *Ethnologue: Languages of the world*. Dallas, TX: SIL International.

Evans, N. (2007). Standing up your mind: Remembering in Dalabon. In M. Amberber (Ed.), *The Language of Memory in a Cross-Linguistic Perspective* (pp. 67–96). Amsterdam: John Benjamins.

Evans, N. & Levinson, S. C. (2009). The myth of language universals: Language diversity and its importance for cognitive science. *Behavioral Brain Sciences*, 32(5): 429–448.

Fernández, J. (2017). The intentional objects of memory. In S. Bernecker & K. Michaelian (Eds.), *The Routledge Handbook of Philosophy of Memory* (pp. 88–99). Abingdon: Routledge.

Frise, M. (2015). Epistemology of memory. *Internet Encyclopedia of Philosophy*. https://iep.utm.edu/epis-mem/.

Furlong, E. J. (1948). Memory. *Mind*, 57: 16–44.

Furlong, E. J. (1951). *A Study in Memory: A Philosophical Essay*. London: Nelson.

Furlong, E. J. (1970). Mr. Urmson on memory and imagination. *Mind*, 79(313): 137–138.

Gabrieli, J. D. E., Fleischman, D. A., Keane, M. M., Reminger, S. L., & Morrel, F. (1995). Double dissociation between memory systems underlying explicit and implicit memory in the human brain. *Psychological Science*, 6(2): 72–82.

Gallistel, C. R. & King, A. P. (2010). *Memory and the Computational Brain*. Hoboken, NJ: Wiley-Blackwell.

Garry, M., Manning, C. G., Loftus, E. F., & Sherman, S. J. (1996). Imagination inflation: Imagining a childhood event inflates confidence that it occurred. *Psychonomic Bulletin and Review*, 3: 208–214.

Gershman, S. (2022). The molecular memory code and synaptic plasticity: A synthesis. *Biosystems*, 104825.

Gilboa, A. & Moscovitch, M. (2021). No consolidation without representation: Correspondence between neural and psychological representations in recent and remote memory. *Neuron*, 109(14): 2239–2255.

Glenberg, A. M. (1997). What memory is for. *Behavioral and Brain Sciences*, 20(1): 1–55.

Hardt, O., Einarsson, E. Ö., & Nader, K. (2010). A bridge over troubled water: Reconsolidation as a link between cognitive and neuroscientific memory research traditions. *Annual Review of Psychology*, 61: 141–167.

Hassabis, D., Kumaran, D., Vann, S. D., & Maguire, E. A. (2007). Patients with hippocampal amnesia cannot imagine new experiences. *Proceedings of the National Academy of Sciences*,104: 1726–1731.

Hazlett, A. (2010). The myth of factive verbs. *Philosophy and Phenomenological Research*, 80(3): 497–522.

Heil, J. (1978). Traces of things past. *Philosophy of Science*, 45(1), 60–72.

Henke, K. (2010). A model for memory systems based on processing modes rather than consciousness. *Nature Reviews Neuroscience*, 11(7): 523–532.

Hobbes, T. (1651/1994). *Leviathan*. Cambridge, MA: Hackett.

Holland, R. F. (1954). The empiricist theory of memory. *Mind*, 63(252): 464–486.

Hume, D. (1739/1978). *A Treatise of Human Nature*. Oxford: Oxford University Press.

Hurley, S. L. (1998). *Consciousness in Action*. Cambridge, MA: Harvard University Press.

Hutto, D. D. (2022). Remembering without a trace? Moving beyond trace minimalism. In A. Sant'Anna, C. McCarroll, & K. Michaelian (Eds.), *Current Controversies in Philosophy of Memory* (pp. 61–81). Abingdon: Routledge.

James, W. (1890). *The Principles of Psychology*. New York: Henry Holt & Co.

Janssen, S. M. J., Chessa, A. G., & Murre, J. M. J. (2006). Memory for time: How people date events. *Memory and Cognition*, 34(1): 138–147.

Jelinek, E. (1995). Quantification in Straits Salish. In E. W. Bach (Ed.), *Quantification in Natural Languages* (pp. 487–540). Dordrecht: Springer.

Josselyn, S. A., Köhler, S., & Frankland, P. W. (2015). Finding the engram. *Nature Reviews Neuroscience*, 16(9), 521–534.

Klein, S. B., Cosmides, L., Tooby, J., & Chance, S. (2002). Decisions and the evolution of memory: Multiple systems, multiple functions. *Psychological Review*, 109: 306–329.

Kurtzman, H. S. (1983). Modern conceptions of memory. *Philosophy and Phenomenological Research*, 44(1): 1–19.

Laird, J. (1920). *A Study in Realism*. Cambridge: Cambridge University Press.

Langland-Hassan, P. (2022). Propping up the causal theory. *Synthese*, 200(2): 1–27.

Lashley, K. S. (1950). In search of the engram. In Society for Experimental Biology (Ed.), *Physiological Mechanisms in Animal Behavior* (Society's Symposium IV) (pp. 454–482). Cambridge: Academic Press.

Leibniz, G. W. (1714/1989). *Philosophical Writings*. Cambridge, MA: Hackett.

Locke, D. (1971). *Memory*. Garden City, NY: Anchor Books.

Locke, J. (1694/1979). *An Essay Concerning Human Understanding*. Oxford: Oxford University Press.

Loftus, E. F., Miller, D. G., & Burns, H. J. (1978). Semantic integration of verbal information into a visual memory. *Journal of Experimental Psychology: Human Learning and Memory*, 4(1): 19–31.

Loftus, E. F. & Pickrell, J. E. (1995). The formation of false memories. *Psychiatric Annals*, 25: 720–725.

Mahr, J. B. & Csibra, G. (2018). Why do we remember? The communicative function of episodic memory. *Behavioral and Brain Sciences*, 41: e1.

Malcolm, N. (1963). *Knowledge and Certainty*. Ithaca, NY: Cornell University Press.

Malcolm, N. (1977). *Memory and Mind*. Ithaca, NY: Cornell University Press.

Marr, D. (1971). Simple memory: A theory for archicortex. *Philosophical Transactions of the Royal Society of London B: Biological Sciences*, 262 (841): 23–81, https://doi.org/10.1098/rstb.1971.0078.

Martin, C. B. & Deutscher, M. (1966). Remembering. *Philosophical Review*, 75: 161–196.

Martin, M. G. (2001). Out of the past: Episodic recall as retained acquaintance. In C. Hoerl & T. McCormack (Eds.), *Time and Memory: Issues in Philosophy and Psychology* (pp. 257–284). New York: Oxford University Press.

McCarroll, C. (2018). *Remembering from the Outside*. Oxford: Oxford University Press.

McClelland, J. L., McNaughton, B. L., & O'Reilly, R. C. (1995). Why there are complementary learning systems in the hippocampus and neocortex: Insights from the successes and failures of connectionist models of learning and memory. *Psychological Review*, 102: 419–457.

McClelland, J. L., Rumelhart, D. E., & Hinton, G. E. (1986). *The Appeal of Parallel Distributed Processing*. Cambridge, MA: MIT Press.

McDonald, R. J. & White, N. M. (1993). A triple dissociation of memory systems: Hippocampus, amygdala, and dorsal striatum. *Behavioral Neuroscience*, 107(1): 3–22.

McKoon, G., Ratcliff, R., & Dell, G. S. (1986). A critical evaluation of the semantic-episodic distinction. *Journal of Experimental Psychology: Learning, Memory, and Cognition*, 12(2): 295–306.

Merleau-Ponty, M. (1945). *Phenomenologie de la perception*. Paris: Gallimard.

Michaelian, K. (2011). Generative memory. *Philosophical Psychology*, 24(3): 323–342.

Michaelian, K. (2016). *Mental Time Travel: Episodic Memory and Our Knowledge of the Personal Past*. Cambridge, MA: MIT Press.

Michaelian, K. (2020). Confabulating as unreliable imagining: In defence of the simulationist account of unsuccessful remembering. *Topoi*, 39(1): 133–148.

Michaelian, K. (2022). Radicalizing simulationism: Remembering as imagining the (nonpersonal) past. *Philosophical Psychology*, https://doi.org/10.1080/09515089.2022.2082934.

Michaelian, K. & Robins, S. K. (2018). Beyond the causal theory? Fifty years after Martin and Deutscher. In K. Michaelian, D. Debus, & D. Perrin (Eds.), *New Directions in the Philosophy of Memory* (pp. 13–32). New York: Routledge.

Michaelian, K. & Sutton, J. (2017). Memory. In Edward N. Zalta (Ed.), *Stanford Encyclopedia of Philosophy*. https://plato.stanford.edu/archives/sum2017/entries/memory/.

Milner, B. (1962). Les troubles de la memoire accompagnant des lesions hippocampiques bilaterales. *Physiologie de l'hippocampe, 107:* 257–272. Paris: Centre national de la recherche scientifique.

Milner, B., Corkin, S., & Teuber, H. L. (1968). Further analysis of the hippocampal amnesic syndrome: 14-year follow-up study of H. M. *Neuropsychologia*, 6: 215–234.

Moran, A. (2021). Memory disjunctivism: A causal theory. *Review of Philosophy and Psychology*, 13(4): 1097–1117.

Moscovitch, M. (2007). Memory: Why the engram is elusive. In H. L. Roediger III, Y. Dudai, & S. M. Fitzpatrick (Eds.), *Science of Memory: Concepts* (pp. 17–21). Oxford: Oxford University Press.

Munsat, S. (1966). *The Concept of Memory*. New York: Random House.

Murray, E. A., Wise, S. P., & Graham, K. S. (2017). *Evolution of Memory Systems: Ancestors, Anatomy, and Adaptations*. Oxford. Oxford University Press.

Nadel, L. & Moscovitch, M. (1997). Memory consolidation, retrograde amnesia and the hippocampal complex. *Current Opinion in Neurobiology*, 7(2): 217–227.

Nader, K. & Hardt, O. (2009). A single standard for memory: The case for reconsolidation. *Nature Reviews Neuroscience*, 10(3): 224–234.

O'Kane, G., Kensinger, E. A., & Corkin, S. (2004). Evidence for semantic learning in profound amnesia: An investigation with patient HM. *Hippocampus*, 14(4): 417–425.

O'Keefe, J. & Nadel, L. (1978). *The Hippocampus As a Cognitive Map*. Oxford: Oxford University Press.

Perrin, D. (2016). Asymmetries in subjective time. In K. Michaelian, S. B. Klein, & K. K. Szpunar (Eds.), *Seeing the Future: Theoretical Perspectives on Future-Oriented Mental Time Travel* (pp. 39–61). New York: Oxford University Press.

Perrin, D. (2018). A case for procedural causality in episodic recollection. In K. Michaelian, D. Debus, & D. Perrin (Eds.), *New Directions in the Philosophy of Memory* (pp. 33–51). Abingdon: Routledge.

Perrin, D. & Michaelian, K. (2017). Memory as mental time travel. In S. Bernecker & K. Michaelian (Eds.), *The Routledge Handbook of Philosophy of Memory* (pp. 228–239). Abingdon: Routledge.

Ranganath, C. & Blumenfeld, R. S. (2005). Doubts about double dissociations between short- and long-term memory. *Trends in Cognitive Science*, 9: 374–380.

Reder, L. M., Park, H., & Kieffaber, P. D. (2009). Memory systems do not divide on consciousness: Reinterpreting memory in terms of activation and binding. *Psychological Bulletin*, 135(1): 23–49.

Reid, T. (1785/1849). *Essays on the Intellectual Powers of Man*. Edinburgh: McLachlan, Stewart, & Co.

Robins, S. K. (2016a). Representing the past: Memory traces and the causal theory of memory. *Philosophical Studies*, 173: 2993–3013.

Robins, S. K. (2016b). Optogenetics and the mechanism of false memory. *Synthese*, 193: 1561–1583.

Robins, S. K. (2017). Memory traces. In S. Bernecker & K. Michaelian (Eds.), *The Routledge Handbook of the Philosophy of Memory* (pp. 76–87). Abingdon: Routledge.

Robins, S. K. (2018). Memory and optogenetic intervention: Separating the engram from the ecphory. *Philosophy of Science*, 85(5): 1078–1089.

Robins, S. K. (2020). Stable engrams and neural dynamics. *Philosophy of Science*, 87(5): 1130–1139.

Robins, S. K. (2022). Episodic memory is not for the future. In A. Sant'Anna, C. McCarroll, & K. Michaelian (Eds.), *Current Controversies in Philosophy of Memory* (pp. 166–184). Abingdon: Routledge.

Roediger, H. L. & McDermott, K. B. (1995). Creating false memories: Remembering words that were not presented in lists. *Journal of Experimental Psychology: Learning, Memory and Cognition*, 21: 803–814.

Rosen, D. A. (1975). An argument for the logical notion of memory trace. *Philosophy of Science*, 42(1): 1–10.

Rowlands, M. (2017). *Memory and the Self: Phenomenology, Science and Autobiography*. Oxford: Oxford University Press.

Rumelhart, D. E., McClelland, J. L., & PDP Research Group (Eds.). (1986). *Parallel Distributed Processing: Explorations in the Microstructure of Cognition, Vol. 1: Foundations*. Cambridge, MA: MIT Press.

Russell, B. (1921). *The Analysis of the Mind*. Abingdon: Routledge.

Ryle, G. (1949). *The Concept of Mind*. London: Hutchinson & Co.

Schacter, D. L. (2008). *Searching for Memory: The Brain, the Mind, and the Past*. New York: Basic Books.

Schacter, D. L., Benoit, R. G., De Brigard, F., & Szpunar, K. K. (2015). Episodic future thinking and episodic counterfactual thinking: Intersections between memory and decisions. *Neurobiology of Learning and Memory*, 117: 14–21.

Schulz, A. W. & Robins, S. (2022). Episodic memory, simulated future planning, and their evolution. *Review of Philosophy and Psychology*, 1–22, https://doi.org/10.1007/s13164-021-00601-1.

Schwartz, A. (2018). Memory and disjunctivism. *Essays in Philosophy*, 19(2), 213–230.

Schwartz, A. (2020). Simulationism and the function(s) of episodic memory. *Review of Philosophy and Psychology*, 11(2): 487–505.

Schwitzgebel, E. (2008). The unreliability of naive introspection. *Philosophical Review*, 117(2): 245–273.

Scoville, W. & Milner, B. (1957). Loss of recent memory after bilateral hippocampal lesions. *Journal of Neurological and Neurosurgical Psychiatry*, 20: 11–12.

Semon, R. W. (1904/1921). *The Mneme*. London: Allen & Unwin.

Shoemaker, S. (1972). Memory. *Encyclopedia of Philosophy*. New York: Macmillan.

Sorabji, R. (1972). *Aristotle on Memory*. London: Duckworth.

Spinoza, B. (1677/1992). *Treatise on the Emendation of Intellect*. Cambridge, MA: Hackett.

Squire, L. R. (1986). Mechanisms of memory. *Science*, 232: 1612–1619.

Squire, L. R. (1992). Memory and the hippocampus: A synthesis from findings with rats, monkeys, and humans. *Psychological Review*, 99: 195–231.

Squires, R. (1969). Memory unchained. *Philosophical Review*, 78(2): 178–196.

Stanley, J. (2011). *Know How*. Oxford: Oxford University Press.

Stout, G. F. (1899). *A Manual of Psychology*. London: W. B. Clive.

Stout, G. F. (1930). In what way is memory-knowledge immediate? In G. F. Stout, *Studies in Philosophy and Psychology* (pp. 166–181) London: McMillian and Co.

Suddendorf, T. & Corballis, M. C. (2007). The evolution of foresight: What is mental time travel and is it unique to humans? *Behavioral and Brain Sciences*, 30: 299–313.

Sutton, J. (1998). *Philosophy and Memory Traces: Descartes to Connectionism*. Cambridge: Cambridge University Press.

Szpunar, K., Watson, J. M., & McDermott, K. B. (2007). Neural substrates of envisioning the future. *Proceedings of the National Academy of Sciences*, 104: 642–647.

Talland, G. A. (1965). *Deranged Memory: A Psychonomic Study of the Amnesic Syndrome*. New York: Academic Press.

Teyler, T. J. & DiScenna, P. (1986). The hippocampal memory indexing theory. *Behavioral Neuroscience*, 100: 147–152.

Tolman, E. C. (1940). Spatial angle and vicarious trial and error. *Journal of Comparative Psychology*, 30(1): 129–135.

Tulving, E. (1972). Episodic and semantic memory. In E. Tulving & W. Donaldson (Eds.), *Organization of Memory* (pp. 381–403). New York: Academic Press.

Tulving, E. (1983). *Elements of Episodic Memory*. Oxford: Oxford University Press.

Tulving, E. (1985). Memory and consciousness. *Canadian Psychology*, 26: 1–12.

Umanath, S. & Coane, J. H. (2020). Face validity of remembering and knowing: Empirical consensus and disagreement between participants and researchers. *Perspectives on Psychological Science*, 15(6): 1400–1422.

Urmson, J. O. (1967). Memory and imagination. *Mind*, 76(301): 83–91.

Van Fraassen, B. C. (1980). *The Scientific Image*. Oxford: Oxford University Press.

Vargha-Khadem, F., Gadian, D. G., Watkins, K. E., et al. (1997). Differential effects of early hippocampal pathology on episodic and semantic memory. *Science*, 277(5324): 376–380.

Vendler, Z. (1972). *Res cogitans*: An essay in rational psychology. *Foundations of Language*, 14(3): 459–461.

Von Leyden, W. (1961). *Remembering: A Philosophical Problem*. London: Duckworth.

Vosgerau, G. (2010). Memory and content. *Consciousness and Cognition*, 19 (3): 838–846.

Warrington, E. K. & McCarthy, R. A. (1988). The fractionation of retrograde amnesia. *Brain and Cognition*, 7(2): 184–200.

Warrington, E. K. & Shallice, T. (1969). The selective impairment of auditory verbal short-term memory. *Brain*, 92: 885–896.

Werning, M. (2020). Predicting the past from minimal traces: Episodic memory and its distinction from imagination and preservation. *Review of Philosophy and Psychology*, 11(2): 301–333.

Werning, M. & Cheng, S. (2017). Taxonomy and unity of memory. In S. Bernecker & K. Michaelian (Eds.), *The Routledge Handbook of Philosophy of Memory* (pp. 7–20). Abingdon: Routledge.

Wittgenstein, L. (1953). *Philosophical Investigations*. Oxford: Basil Blackwell.

Wittgenstein, L. (1980). *Remarks on the Philosophy of Psychology*. Oxford: Blackwell.

Woozley, A. D. (1949). *Theory of Knowledge*. London: Hutchinson.

Zemach, E. M. (1968). A definition of memory. *Mind*, 77(308): 526–536.

Zeman, A. & Butler, C. (2010). Transient epileptic amnesia. *Current Opinion in Neurology*, 23(6): 610–616.

Dedication

Dedicated to my father, Luis, and to my mother, Teresita

Milton Keynes UK
Ingram Content Group UK Ltd.
UKHW020042141223
434277UK00011B/59